The Encyclopedia of
GREETING CARD
Tools & Techniques

Fond greeting!

Susan Pickering Rothamel

The Encyclopedia of GREETING CARD Tools & Techniques

Susan Pickering Rothamel

LARK CRAFTS

An Imprint of Sterling Publishing Co., Inc.
New York

WWW.LARKCRAFTS.COM

Senior Editor:
Ray Hemachandra

Editor:
Larry Shea

Assistant Editors:
Mark Bloom
Cassie Moore

Art Director:
Kathleen Holmes

Assistant Art Director:
Avery Johnson

Photographers:
Stewart O'Shields
Shawn Hall

Cover Designer:
Travis Medford

The Library of Congress has cataloged the hardcover edition as follows:

Rothamel, Susan Pickering.
    Encyclopedia of greeting cards tools and techniques   /   Susan Pickering Rothamel.
        p. cm.
    Includes index.
    ISBN-13: 978-1-60059-029-0 (hc-plc with jacket : alk. paper)
    ISBN-10: 1-60059-029-2 (hc-plc with jacket : alk. paper)
    1.   Greeting cards.   2. Handicraft.   I.   Title.
TT872.R67 2008
745.594'1--dc22

                                    2007050641

10 9 8 7 6 5 4 3 2

Published by Lark Crafts, An Imprint of Sterling Publishing Co., Inc.
387 Park Avenue South, New York, NY 10016

First Paperback Edition 2011
Text and illustrations © 2011, Susan Pickering Rothamel
Photography © 2011, Lark Crafts unless otherwise specified

Distributed in Canada by Sterling Publishing, c/o Canadian Manda Group,
165 Dufferin Street Toronto, Ontario, Canada M6K 3H6

Distributed in the United Kingdom by GMC Distribution Services,
Castle Place, 166 High Street, Lewes, East Sussex, England BN7 1XU

Distributed in Australia by Capricorn Link (Australia) Pty Ltd.,
P.O. Box 704, Windsor, NSW 2756 Australia

The written instructions, photographs, designs, patterns, and projects in this volume are intended for the personal use of the reader and may be reproduced for that purpose only. Any other use, especially commercial use, is forbidden under law without written permission of the copyright holder.

Every effort has been made to ensure that all the information in this book is accurate. However, due to differing conditions, tools, and individual skills, the publisher cannot be responsible for any injuries, losses, and other damages that may result from the use of the information in this book.

If you have questions or comments about this book, please contact:
Lark Crafts
67 Broadway
Asheville, NC 28801
828-253-0467

Manufactured in China

ISBN 13: 978-1-60059-029-0 (hardcover) 978-1-4547-0121-7 (paperback)

For information about custom editions, special sales, and premium and corporate purchases, please contact the Sterling Special Sales Department at 800-805-5489 or specialsales@sterlingpub.com.

For information about desk and examination copies available to college and university professors, requests must be submitted to academic@larkbooks.com. Our complete policy can be found at www.larkcrafts.com.

Contents

Introduction

THIS BOOK is a true labor of love. My goal was to gather together all the history, terminology, how-to advice, and inspiration you need to appreciate the great tradition of making and sending cards and to become a cardmaker yourself. The timeline that starts off the book covers everything from the first Valentine in 270 AD to the most recent developments in the greeting-card industry. The alphabetical journey that follows defines and explains techniques (*Dry Embossing* and *Gilding*, for example), tools (*Corrugator, Stylus*), types of cards (*Fold-Out, Repurposed*), and much more. Many of the entries include a "How-to Basics" section that teaches you how the techniques are actually done. Examples of contemporary and historical cards add explanation and inspiration to the topics covered.

For many people, collecting the mail is just another routine task in a busy day. But imagine leafing through the bills, advertisements, and credit-card solicitations only to find a square white envelope. Your name is handwritten on it, and there's a real postage stamp in the upper right-hand corner. Anticipation mounting, you pause and say to yourself, "Wow, someone sent me a card!"

Sending a card is almost as nice as receiving one. In truth, I used to wonder if my family and friends really appreciated my handmade cards. But the few times I've sent store-bought cards, they've been quick to ask if everything is okay, as if getting an ordinary card from me means something is wrong. It's a nice feeling to know that they attach value to my humble gifts.

As you'll discover in this book, handmade cards have a long and admirable history. Today, unfortunately, many people think of greeting cards only as what they see in those racks at the local drugstore. Over the years, making cards has been transformed from an individual, relatively rare pursuit into a big business. There are approximately 3,000 card publishers in the United States alone. Americans purchase nearly seven billion greeting cards every year, generating nearly $7.5 billion in retail sales.

With today's rising interest in paper crafts of all types, more and more people are bringing the greeting card back to its origins as a unique item designed to express truly personal sentiments. The craft industry provides an abundance of paper materials and a myriad of cardmaking embellishments, from ribbons and beads to stickers and rubberstamps. An amazing array of materials is available. You only need to look for a large craft store, an independent

paper shop, or even your local grocery store. Today, anyone can create a greeting card from the comfort of home.

You'll be astounded by the hundreds of creative cards displayed in this book. I can't begin to thank all of the artists who kindly allowed me to share their cards. Some cardmakers are enthusiastic crafters who just enjoy the cardmaking process and use fairly traditional materials. Others are fabulous designers and artists who labor over each card, developing special techniques and carefully composing their color schemes.

A number of these cardmakers are featured in the artist profiles sprinkled throughout the book. You'll meet Dee Gruenig, a multi-talented cardmaker, instructor, and entrepreneur who truly can be considered the "Queen of Stamping," as well as Cy Thiewes, an artist who was inspired in her retirement to recycle her watercolor paintings into brilliantly vibrant cards. All of the artists whose work you'll see here are proudly carrying on the centuries-old tradition of handmade cards.

Traditions are meant to be passed along. I hope that the words and images that follow inspire you to join in the tradition yourself—or, if you're already a seasoned cardmaker, to expand your horizons and try out some of the many enticing methods for creating cards you'll find here.

Most of the designs in the book are relatively easy to produce right at your own kitchen table. Use what you have at hand, such as pressed leaves and flowers, scrapbooking materials, computer paper, and rubberstamps. If you are a fine artist, think "off the wall" and consider the card stock as your canvas. Adapt your more formal art supplies, and use them to start your own cardmaking tradition.

The soup-to-nuts information—actually, *Accordion Fold* to *Wrinkling*—you'll find in this encyclopedia will help you begin and provide hundreds of ideas to inspire your creativity. Making your own cards is extremely satisfying, and one day you may see your work framed on a friend's wall or saved in a scrapbook album. If so, you'll know your gift—a humble, heartfelt handmade card—will be treasured forever.

The History of Greeting Cards

A Sumerian tablet

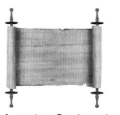

An ancient Greek parchment

BC

Sumerians invent cuneiform writing. Using a blunt reed to make cuneiform ("wedge-shaped") impressions on clay tablets, they attain both a method of record keeping and a message delivery system.

2000–2500 BC

The Egyptians invent hieroglyphics and papyrus, a paper-like substance, which allows them to convey messages and greetings much easier than using clay tablets.

1500–1000 BC

The Aztecs paint intricate designs on prepared bark. These petroglyph messages are carried by runners to recipients.

600 BC

The Greeks develop long scrolls of parchment made of goat skin, which is more durable than papyrus.

105 AD

China produces an economical paper made of a variety of materials. Can greeting cards be far behind?

270

According to legend, St. Valentine, a third-century Roman priest, performs secret marriages against the order of Emperor Claudius II. The Emperor, who believes single soldiers are more likely to join his army, has Valentine arrested. Before his execution on February 14, the priest sends a note to the jailer's daughter, signing it "From Your Valentine."

496

Pope Gelasius authorizes February 14 to honor St. Valentine as the patron saint of lovers. According to the *Catholic Encyclopedia*, there are at least three early Christian saints by that name: the priest in Rome, a bishop in Terni, and a missionary in Africa. According the the book, the three die or are martyred on February 14.

500–1000

Western cultures still copy books by hand onto animal skin parchment. The process is too long and costly for greeting cards.

593

China invents the first printing press.

600–750

Greeting cards make another evolutionary step forward when papermaking techniques spread throughout Asia and the Middle East. The Japanese refine the art.

901

The Chinese use wood blocks to print pictures and text. The Japanese begin the art form of origami, linking it with their message-sending tradition.

1238

Spain develops the first paper mills, but not the first greeting cards.

1400s

Handmade paper greeting cards are exchanged in Europe. Germans print seasonal New Year's greetings called Andachtsbilder from woodcuts. A devotional picture, most often decorated with the Christ Child, includes the sentiment "A good and blessed year."

1415

The first written valentine may have come from Charles, Duke of Orleans, who wrote romantic verses to his wife while imprisoned.

1420

John Lydgate composes a Valentine's Day greeting for Henry V to give to Catherine of Valois:

> Seynte Valentine of custome yeere by yeere
> Men have an usance, in this regioun
> To loke and serche Cupides kalendar,
> And chose theyr choyse by grete affeccioun,
> Such has been move with Cupides nocioun,
> Takying theyre choyse as theyre sort doth falle;
> But I love oon whiche excelleth alle.

1450

In Europe, Johann Gutenberg invents the first printing press with movable type, which allows him to economically print many copies of the Bible.

1470

Woodcuts are introduced in Europe to illustrate the printed word.

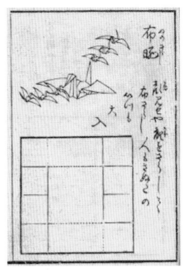

A page from *Hiden Senbazuru Orikata*, the oldest origami book in the world, ca. 1797

A German woodcut from an Andachtsbilder

The 1450 Gutenberg press

1476

William Caxton becomes the first printer in Westminster, England.

1477

Margery Brews sends her fiancé a Valentine Card. It is the oldest known greeting card still in existence. Here is a portion:

> *Unto my ryght welebelovyd Voluntyn, John Paston, Squyer, be this bill delyvered, &c.*
> Ryght reverent and wurschypfull, and my ryght welebeloved Volutyne,
> I recomande me unto yowe, ffull hertely desyring to here of yowr welefare,
> whech I beseche Almyghty God long for to preserve un to Hys plesur,
> and yowr herts desyre. And yf it please yowe to here of my welefar,
> I am not in good heele of body, nor of herte, nor schall be tyll I her ffrom yowe;
> For there wottys no creature what peyn that I endure,
> And for to be deede, I dare it not dyscure [discover].

1500

European presses begin printing books.

GREETING CARD FUN FACTS

U.S. consumers purchase approximately seven billion greeting cards each year, generating nearly $7.5 billion in retail sales.

More than 90 percent of all U.S. households buy greeting cards, with the average household purchasing 30 individual cards in a year.

In 1954, Americans sent about two billion Christmas cards. Today, the yearly figure stands at close to four billion, or an average of 20 cards per person.

Sixty-two percent of people feel inspired to send someone a card if they have received one from that person.

Women purchase more than 80 percent of all greeting cards.

Women are more likely than men to buy several cards at once. However, men generally spend more on a single card.

The two categories of greeting cards are seasonal and everyday. Sales are split approximately 50-50 between the two types.

The most popular seasonal cards are Christmas (60 percent), Valentine's Day (25 percent), Mother's Day (4 percent), Easter (3 percent), and Father's Day (3 percent).

The most popular everyday cards are birthday (60 percent), anniversary (8 percent), get well (7 percent), friendship (6 percent), and sympathy cards (6 percent).

There are an estimated 3,000 greeting card publishers in the U.S. alone.

The United Kingdom is the world leader in sending greetings cards, spending more than £1 billion each year.

Until Christmas 1961, the UK Post Office used to deliver cards on Christmas morning.

Among industrialized countries, the average person receives more than 20 cards per year, about one-third of which are birthday cards.

Source: *Some of the above facts are courtesy of the Greeting Card Association (www.greetingcard.org).*

1639
The Boston, Massachusetts, tavern of Richard Fairbanks, becomes the first repository for overseas mail.

1775
New Year's, Valentine's Day, and Christmas cards become popular. Commercially made, they feature mechanical, pop-up, and filigree effects.

On July 26, members of the Second Continental Congress agree "... that a Postmaster General be appointed for the United States, and be paid a salary of 1,000 dollars per year." Benjamin Franklin becomes the first Postmaster General under the Continental Congress.

1789
Mass-produced Valentine's Day cards become available.

Samuel Osgood becomes the first Postmaster General under the U.S. Constitution.

1796
Johann Nepomuk Franz Alois Senefelder of Prague, Czechoslovakia, perfects a chemical printing process the French dub "lithography." Within 25 years, European printers are mass-producing lithographed devotional prints. By 1825, the new technology is common in the United States. By the 1840s, Senefelder's color process—known as "chromolithography"—gives an added dimension to small die-cuts and greeting cards.

Johann Nepomuk Franz Alois Senefelder, inventer of lithography

1825
The U.S. 'dead letter' office is formed.

1829
The U.S. Postmaster General, William T. Barry of Kentucky, joins Andrew Jackson's President's Cabinet.

1830s
Esther Howland, known as the Mother of the Valentine, makes fancy Valentines with real lace, ribbons, and colorful pictures known as "scrap."

Esther sent ten prototype designs to her brother, a salesman for a stationery company. The response was enormous—in New England alone, he took orders for over $5000. Esther purchased color pictures, paper lace, and real ribbon. Recruiting her friends, she set up an assembly line: one cut pictures, another adhered flowers, and a third attached ribbon or lace. Artisans painted floral elements on silk—sometimes adding a small mirror—as embellishments.

One of Esther Howland's original Valentine's Day cards

Sold for fifty cents, each Valentine was a fantasy of romance and inspiration. No one could compete with Esther's style or quality. She was among the first entrepreneurs to recognize the potential of assembly-line production. Her business showed profits of $100,000 each year, amazing considering the era. When Whitney Company bought her card line and began machine-producing the cards, Esther's intricate, handmade designs became a thing of the past.

The 1843 Horsley card, courtesy of Hallmark Archives, Hallmark Cards, Inc. John Calcott Horsley became the world's first Christmas card sender when he presented Sir Henry Cole with a signed copy of his original design, bearing the inscription:

> "To his good friend Cole
> Who's a merry young soul
> And a merry young soul is he:
> And may he be for many years to come! Hooray!"

1837

Sir Rowland Hill, Postmaster General of England, proposes reformation of the postal system, including a set rate for postage to be paid by the sender.

1838

U.S. Congress designates railroad postal routes.

1840

Queen Victoria begins sending Christmas cards.

May 1: The world's first postage stamp with an adhesive on the back is issued. Sir Henry Cole designs the black-and-white one-cent stamp with a portrait of Queen Victoria, nicknamed the "Penny Black." It is quickly replaced by the Penny Red because the Postal Service could not distinguish the black cancellation ink over the black stamp. On May 8, a two-penny blue stamp becomes available.

1843

Sir Henry Cole hires artist John Calcott Horsley to design a holiday card for friends and acquaintances. The card is also sold commercially for one shilling each. Since it depicts a family with a small child drinking wine together, some critics claim the card encourages intemperance. About 1,000 cards are printed in black and white and then hand-colored. Originals are extremely rare—only about ten have survived—but you can easily find the 1955 reprints.

1847

July 1: In New York City, the first postage stamps are issued in the United States. The first five-cent stamp depicting Benjamin Franklin and the ten-cent George Washington are released.

1848

The first public mailboxes appear in Russia on December 13. Made of wood and iron, they are often stolen. Future mailboxes are made of cast iron, weighing about 88 pounds (40 kilos). Greeting cards are finally safe.

1851

The earliest American-made Christmas cards are store advertisements by R.H. Pease Great Variety in Albany, New York. The lithograph card depicts Santa Claus with a family enjoying their presents, while a servant sets the table. In subsequent years, the cards show mangers, holly, snowmen, and even Little Red Riding Hood.

1852

Pre-stamped envelopes are introduced. A two-cent stamp in black featuring Andrew Jackson is issued. It is dubbed the "Black Jack."

1854
Perforated stamps are introduced.

1856
Louis Prang becomes known as the Father of the Christmas Card, producing cards at his Boston lithographic shop every year for the holiday.

1860
The four-color, photo-mechanical lithographic printing process evolves. This process revolutionizes the printing industry, providing speedy, cost-effective card printing.

1860s
Charles Bennett, Goodall, and Marcus Ward & Co. begin mass-producing greeting cards.

The US Pony Express is introduced.

1863
The US Postal service unifies postage rates, regardless of distance or pages.

1868
Kate Greenaway designs greeting cards for Marcus Ward. Her subjects consist of children, flowers, and landscapes.

1870
Victorians collect beautifully printed cards and scraps for their parlor albums. Trade cards, issued by businesses to advertise their products, become highly collectible.

1872
The first advertising postcard appears in England.

1873
United States Postal Service begins issuing pre-stamped one-cent post cards.

1875
Louis Prang, a German immigrant, publishes the first line of U.S. Christmas cards.

1881
John Calcott Horsley popularizes Christmas cards.

1889
The Heligoland card is considered the first multi-colored postcard ever printed.

A Louis Prang Christmas card from the 1870s, courtesy of Hallmark Archives, Hallmark Cards, Inc.

An 1868 Kate Greenaway Christmas card, courtesy of Dwayne Hill. www.kategreenawaycards.com

A trade card from the Woolson Spice Co., from the collection of Susan Pickering Rothamel

An 1895 "Little Girl" postcard from the collection of Susan Pickering Rothamel

The 1905 Sapirstein logo

A 1906 Ellen H. Clapsaddle post-card from the collection of Susan Pickering Rothamel

1891

In Norfolk, Nebraska, brothers Rollie and William Hall buy the Norfolk Post Card Company bookstore. In 1894, they begin selling postcards wholesale.

1893

The first commemorative U.S. postage stamps are introduced.

1898

Congress ends the U.S. Postal Service's monopoly for printing postcards, passing the Private Mailing Card Act. The new law allows private publishers and printers to produce postcards to be mailed for one cent (the same rate as government postcards), instead of two cents. This was perhaps the most important event in making the cards more popular.

Postcards still have an "undivided back." Writing is allowed only on the front side of the card.

Early 1900s

"Real Photo" postcards are introduced, on film stock paper. While most "Real Photo" postcards are advertising and trade cards, many depict entertainers and portraits of family members.

1901

On December 24, the U.S. begins using the words "Post Card" on the back of the card and writing is still only allowed on the front.

1902

England begins printing divided-back postcards.

1905

Jacob Sapirstein, a young Polish immigrant, arrives in Cleveland, Ohio. He borrows $50 to buy German penny postcards, selling them to drug stores, novelty shops, and confectioners. His sons Irving, Morris, and Harry—as well as his daughter Bernice—help organize inventory, stuff fancy post-cards into envelopes, and make deliveries to accounts.

1906

Eastman Kodak enters the marketplace with photo and lithographed greeting cards.

Ellen H. Clapsaddle's artwork is published by the Wolf Company, an outlet for the International Art Company. According to the Greeting Card Association, Clapsaddle is a pioneer and considered the most prolific of all postcard and greeting card artists. Sadly, Clapsaddle died unknown and penniless the day before her 69th birthday.

1967

American Greetings debuts Holly Hobby, the first licensed property launched by Those Characters from Cleveland, Inc. (TCFC, Inc.), an American Greetings subsidiary. From this come other licensed characters, such as Strawberry Shortcake, Care Bears, and the Get Along Gang.

1968

Priority Mail, a subclass of First-Class Mail, is introduced.

1970

Express Mail begins on an experimental basis.

1971

The United States Postal Service (U.S.P.S.) begins. The Postmaster General is no longer a Cabinet position.

1972

Postage stamps become available by U.S. mail.

1980

New postal standards require envelopes and postcards to be at least 3½ inches (8.9 cm) high and 5 inches (12.7 cm) long.

Greeting card manufacturers develop a three-dimensional card—uniquely presented as the gift itself—that can be sent flat through the mail.

1983

ZIP + 4 is introduced.

The American Greetings logo, courtesy of American Greetings Corporation.

A vintage greeting card, used with permission from the Moore Collection, Houston, Texas

1985

American Greetings acquires Dallas-based Drawing Board Greetings, Inc. The acquired company later becomes Carlton Cards, Inc., USA.

1986

At the age of 101, Jacob Sapirstein celebrates the Silver Anniversary of American Greetings by unveiling the "Rose Logo" as part of its corporate identity.

1988

The Greeting Card Association initiates the Louie Awards to celebrate creative excellence in the greeting card industry. Entries are judged on a ten-point scale for criteria that include Imagination, Impact, Artistry, Harmony, Sendability, and Value, with cards in each category divided by price.

1992

Stamps are now sold through automatic teller machines.

GREETING CARD TIPS

Make sending a card or two a weekly habit instead of an occasional afterthought.

While e-cards are easy to send, they rarely reach the heart of their recipient. Take the time to send the real thing.

Personalize the message. Even if a sentiment is pre-printed, add your own words at the bottom or a longer note on the inside.

Always date your cards so that future generations will know the month and year treasured cards were sent.

Instead of using address labels and metered postage, use a stamp and handwrite—or even use an old-fashioned typewriter to type—the address on the envelope.

When complimenting someone for a job well done, sending congratulations, or just saying "I'm thinking of you," be specific and tell the person exactly why you're sending a card. ("Congratulations! Your patients are going to have the best care with you as their nurse.")

Always sign the card, even if your name is printed.

Keep your signature informal—no titles for business associates and no last names for family or friends.

Include your return address. Doing so not only complies with postal service regulations, but also helps your friends keep their mailing lists up-to-date.

Don't wait for a special occasion or a reason to connect. Send an unexpected card for no particular reason. A "thinking of you" or "just because" card can be one of the best ways to show someone you care.

1994

Hallmark invests in Aesop, a domestic Japanese stationary manufacturer. (In 1997, Hallmark increases its share in the company up to 100 percent. In the same year there is a name change, to Nihon Hallmark.)

The card most often sent in Japan is the New Year's greeting card. Next in popularity is the summer greeting card, sent to say "Best wishes" to the recipient. People send dozens of cards to friends and family, handwriting a message.

1996

American Greetings launches its site on the World Wide Web, featuring paper greeting cards, electronic cards, candy, flowers, and gifts, including Egreetings.com and BlueMountain.com.

2000

Gibson joins American Greetings, combining the world's two largest publicly held greeting card companies.

2007

May 14: After increasing the rate 13 times in 32 years, the U.S. Postal Service introduces a 42-cent first-class stamp.

The U.S. Postal Service introduces "The Forever Stamp." On sale on April 12 at 41 cents, customers can begin using it on May 14. Even if the price of postage should increase, the Forever Stamp can be used without additional postage.

On August 8, AmericanGreetings.com launches a Web-to-Mobile greeting card service in the U.S. This new technology enables e-cards to be delivered to cell phones.

Hallmark's artist Gary Head at work, courtesy of Hallmark Cards, Inc.

The American Greetings Corporation World Headquarters, Cleveland, Ohio, 2007. Reproduced with permission from American Greetings Corporation

AUTHOR'S NOTE

With appreciation, I wish to thank these companies and organizations for their enormous cooperation in providing much of the valuable information contained in this timeline, as well as providing, or granting the rights to reproduce, many of these historical photographs.

American Greetings
www.americangreetings.com

Hallmark
www.hallmark.com

United States Postal Service
www.usps.com

ACCORDION FOLDING

A card making technique where each fold runs in the opposite direction to the previous fold, creating a pleated or fanlike effect. *See also* Fold-Out Card.

Accordion folding adds dimension and interest, whether making smaller, carefully ruled, uniform folds or larger asymmetrical folds. For best results, use a bone folder to crease and smooth your paper.

These tri-fold accordion cards provide ample space for words and design elements.

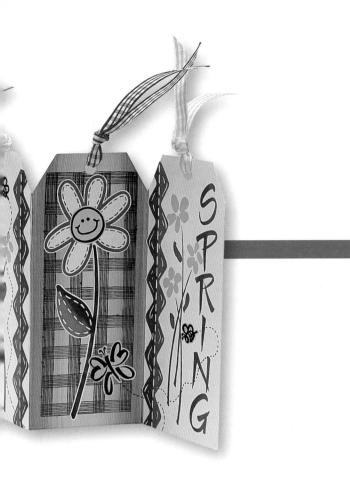

ACETATE

A clear or frosted vinyl sheet used to cover the top of card fronts. The acetate may include designs and words. Be sure to select the correct acetate for inkjet or laser printers.

Print the image directly onto acetate. Then place it over a painted—or as shown here, gilded—background.

Place a botanical image printed on acetate onto card stock with a square, die-cut aperture. When opened, the card resembles a stained glass window.

ACID-FREE

A material with a pH of 7.0 to 9.5, which indicates that it contains no mobile or available acid ions for a chemical reaction. Over time, materials may naturally become acidic by absorption through the atmosphere or by coming in contact with acidic materials.

ACROSTIC CARD

In the 1860s and 1870s publishers such as Marcus Ward, Charles Goodall, and Louis Prang printed Valentine's Day and Christmas cards using a mix of words and images to form sentences. The card's recipient solved the puzzle to reveal the message.

ACID REDUCER

Any product that neutralizes the acid content in paper.

ACRYLIC ADHESIVE

Nonflammable, waterproof, and applied without mixing, this adhesive dries clear and bonds to most surfaces, including slightly oily or porous surfaces. Bonds occur in 30 to 60 seconds, with permanent strength reached in 45 minutes. *See also* Adhesives.

This snowman card has been repurposed from a long-saved pile of cards. Christmas wrap, sparkling green and sporting the Merry Merry theme, is the perfect backdrop for him, once the ratty card edges have been cropped. Small brads reinforced with mica rings provide colorful, contrasting textural elements. Acrylic adhesive has been used to adhere each layer together.

ACRYLIC PAINT

A fast-drying pigment suspended in an acrylic polymer that offers varying levels of opacity and translucency. Acrylic paints are water soluble when wet and become an insoluble film when dry. *See also* Paint.

These charming acrylic-painted holiday cards were once much larger. Now, having been cut, mounted, and essentially reworked, the new cards still retain the artist's original work as the focal point.

ADHESIVE

A substance that comes in liquid, solid, cement, paste, and other forms used to adhere one element to another. Card makers should use non-yellowing, flexible, non-brittle adhesives, and avoid cellulose and starch glues, rubber cement, paper cement, high- or low-temperature glue sticks, vegetable glues, epoxy, animal glues, and wood glues.

Dry and film adhesives

Dry or Film Adhesive—These include any pressure-sensitive, acrylic-based film or tape product. Firm pressure helps develop adhesive contact and improves bond strength. When these adhesives are properly used, bond strength will increase over time. *See also* ATG, Glue Stick, Repositionable Adhesive, and Spray Adhesive.

Types of liquid adhesives

Liquid Adhesive—Permanent and repositionable adhesives are available in bottles, sticks, and pens with thick- or thin-tipped applicators. Liquid adhesives work best for collage and assemblage techniques that require attaching small items such as punches or die-cut letters and dimensional items such as beads and buttons. *See also* Acrylic, Cyanoacrylate, Dimensional Adhesives and Cements, and Polyvinyl Acetate (PVA).

AGING AND DISTRESSING

Techniques that give objects or papers a vintage or antique effect, including ready-made patterned papers, cardstock, photos, embellishments, or found objects. *See also* Shabby Chic and Wrinkling.

Color Aging—Use colored chalks, colored pencils, ink pens, and food items, such as coffee grounds, tea, vegetables, or juices, to color torn edges or highlight a particular word or quote.

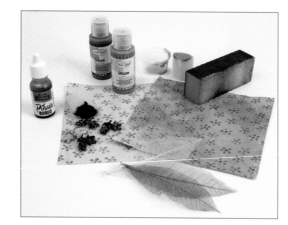

HOW-TO BASICS: **COLOR AGING**

1. Soak, sponge, or use cotton swabs or tissues to wet the paper.

2. Start with a light touch and apply more if needed.

3. Lightly sponge, spritz, or brush earth-tone-colored inks, whitewash glazes, or chalks onto pre-printed and hand-stamped paper, leaves, and hardware to provide cards with a vintage or nostalgic feeling.

Air-Dry Clay

A group of clays that dry without the addition of heat. Always check the manufacturer's packaging to be sure that the clay is acid-free and suitable for paper crafts. Air-dry clays are more brittle and fragile than other varieties of clay. *See also* Clay.

An air-dry clay tablet mounted on a card makes an ordinary card extraordinary.

Album

A blank book used to store photographs, greeting cards, and memorabilia. *See also* Card Album.

Altered Art

In this contemporary art form, recycled objects originally intended for practical purposes, such as books, advertising, and photographs, are turned into works of art by any creative means.

Andachtsbilder

A German New Year's greeting from the 15th century, commonly made from copper plates as well as hand-colored woodcuts. Andachtsbilder are not greeting cards in the traditional sense, but pictures with Christian themes that were shared as gifts.

Angel Company

A term identifying any company that allows a consumer to use its rubberstamp or paper images to create one-of-a-kind products for resale. Policies vary widely, so you'll need to contact each manufacturer about copyright policies.

ANNIVERSARY CARD

A card sent to commemorate a past wedding, either your own or someone else's. These cards tend to emphasize the love or bond between two people. Here are some samples to inspire you. *See also* Special Occasion Card.

ANTI-STATIC PAD

A small bag filled with a static-inhibiting powder. Rubbing a paper surface with the pad reduces static electricity, keeping stray embossing-powder granules from being accidentally heated. It is also used by calligraphers to prevent inks from bleeding into the paper due to static electricity. Anti-static pads are used to reduce static electricity from the acetate windows in shaker boxes.

APERTURE

A die-cut opening or window of any shape in a card.

Whether using the cardstock itself, overlays or even mica tile, an aperture usually frames the focal point or the greeting.

BARGELLO

A style borrowed from needlework techniques in which paper strips are adhered in horizontal sets, then cut and arranged in vertical steps to produce interesting geometric designs that often have an undulating look.

HOW-TO BASICS: BARGELLO

1. Select complementary papers that suit the occasion, and cut them into varying widths.

2. Lay the strips on an adhesive sheet or tape them from behind so the long edges touch.

3. Cut the strips vertically. Stagger the strips, taping them together on the back to form a pattern.

4. Mount the completed piece onto the card.

BATIK

A method of dyeing borrowed from an Indonesian textile technique in which a pattern is drawn with wax on paper. The paper is dipped into inks, dyes, or watercolors, and the wax prevents the color from penetrating the pattern areas. You can obtain multicolored and blended effects by scraping off the initial wax pattern and repeating the dyeing process several times.

HOW-TO BASICS: **BATIK**

1. Select a light-colored paper. (Papers with cotton fibers work best.)

2. Cover your work area with newspaper.

3. Draw a design using an unlit candle, a crayon, or paraffin wax. Each provides a different effect.

4. Crumple the paper into a ball once you've drawn the design.

5. Smooth out the paper, and dip it in a shallow pan filled with a light-colored ink or dye. Wait for the paper to completely absorb the color.

6. Allow the paper to dry thoroughly.

7. If desired, add wax patterns over the inked areas. Dip the paper into the ink again, this time using a darker shade.

8. Allow the paper to dry.

9. Remove the wax by scraping it off with a credit card or by ironing the paper between sheets of newspaper.

You can create distinctive-looking cards with batik, a technique more commonly used with clothing, fabrics, and pillows. Small batiks make charming framable cards.

Bead

A small decorative object pierced for threading or stringing made from glass, polymer, wood, plastic, or other material. *See also* Microbead.

Beads add appeal—and depth—to greeting cards. With the endless variety readily available, you will never run out of ideas for beaded cards.

BIRTHDAY CARD

A card sent to celebrate a birthday. Young or old, your friends and relatives will be touched when they receive a handmade card on their birthday. Here are samples to stir your creative juices. *See also* Special Occasion Card.

Look who's turning 50!

happy
happy
birthday

happy

BLEACH

A technique using household bleach to discolor or alter card stock by removing color from the paper.

CAUTION—Bleach is very strong-smelling. If you are sensitive to chemicals, ventilate your work area well or work outdoors. Read all safety warnings on the container before use. Also make sure your work surface is protected. This technique is suitable for adults only.

TIP

Creating card designs with bleach is fun and innovative. Every paper will perform differently, and some barely work at all. Experimentation is important.

HOW-TO BASICS: **BLEACH STAMPING**

1. Place a pad of paper towels in a small plastic pan.
2. Pour in enough bleach to dampen the paper towels.
3. Tap your stamp onto the bleach-soaked paper towels.
4. Stamp your paper. It may take several minutes for the bleach to finish processing.
5. Use a heat tool to speed up the process.
6. Wash your stamp in warm, soapy water.

HOW-TO BASICS: **BLEACH STENCILING**

1. Place a pad of paper towels in a small plastic pan.
2. Pour in enough bleach to dampen the paper towels.
3. Use masking tape to fix a stencil firmly to your paper.
4. Dampen a stencil brush or sponge by tapping it in the bleach.
5. Tap the brush gently through the stencil.
6. Carefully lift off the stencil, and wash it in clear water. It may take several minutes for the bleach to finish processing.
7. Use a heat tool to speed up the process.

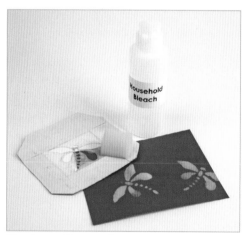

Bleach stenciling supplies

Bleach stamping supplies

BLEED

The migration of ink, paint, or adhesive through or across paper. This process may occur immediately upon application or over time. *Bleed* is also a printer's term used to refer to color (ink, paint, or paper) that runs all the way to the edge of a trimmed page.

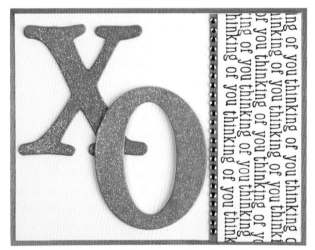

Running color or words right off the edge of a card creates a unique design element. "Bleeding off" can anchor, border, or frame the main design.

▪▪ HOW-TO BASICS: **BLEACH WATERBRUSHING** ▪▪

1. Fill a waterbrush with a mixture of five parts water and one part bleach. Mark the waterbrush, so you use it only for bleach.

2. Paint or draw on colored card stock as you would with a watercolor brush.

3. Use the waterbrush to remove watercolor or ink from any areas you'd like to highlight.

Bleach waterbrushing supplies

BLENDER PEN

A writing utensil filled with a clear fluid formulated to work with solvent-based or water-based markers, watercolors, chalks, or inks. By stroking from the outside in, the fluid pushes a layer of color, causing it to become a lighter shade of the same color. Or, it may mingle with two colors to create a third.

BLIND EMBOSSING

A technique in which a raised image is created on paper under pressure by an engraved metal plate. *See also* Emboss.

Simple mechanical devices are now available with interchangeable stencils giving card makers another alternative to dry emboss. Operating like a punch, they provide just the right pressure to lightweight card stock to produce a small, but perfect image every time.

BLITZER

A hand tool used with standard brush-type markers. Its squeezable bulb releases air over the point of a marker, which creates an airbrush effect.

BLOCKING

See Color Blocking.

BONE FOLDER

A smooth hand tool made of bone or plastic used for folding, scoring, and creasing papers or for pressing out air bubbles and wrinkles when gluing papers and fabrics to other surfaces.

BORDER

A decorative edge, title, line, or design used to sur-round a page. Borders may be self-adhesive stickers, die-cuts, templates, punch-out die cuts, or photos themselves.

Die-cuts and punch-out die cuts add dimension to a card. The possibilities are endless!

Borders come in every conceivable style, material, color, and design. This laser-cut lace border works with all kinds of Victorian, floral, or kitschy designs.

Whimsical, patterned sticker borders even work as a frame. This card actually has multiple layers: a glitter shaker box, coral, a border, and fish and turtle appliqués.

BOTTLE CAP

Easy to find or purchase, bottle caps can be flattened, decorated, and used on frames for photographs, letters, or words. Consider aging, painting, or adding glitter to them to coordinate with any card.

Smashed with a hammer or run over by car tires, bottle caps have long been used as dimensional elements. Here, one is stuffed, along with pretty beads, into a wire mesh tube.

Several bottle caps are evenly smashed and enhanced with die-cuts made with a universal paper crafter's tool.

BOX

A container for storing keepsake cards, available in a myriad of styles. For a bedroom, consider a hatbox or shoebox wallpapered to match the room. For the living room, choose a more formal photograph box or small wooden trunk. *See also* Organization.

BOXED CARD SET

A set of greeting cards often consisting of one particular style, theme, or design created by a single artist.

A small scarf box decorated with a medallion is ideal for a group of medallion cards, each sporting a flower or star. A perfect gift for family, friends, and the elderly, this boxed set needs only a pretty pen and a book of stamps to make it a very special present.

Dragonflies, each different in style, provide a common theme for a boxed set of cards. Even the box top is stamped.

BRAYER

A small hand tool resembling a paint roller used in paper crafts to make background papers or to apply pressure to layers of paper. The most common brayers are made of rubber, hard foam, acrylic, or sponge.

HOW-TO BASICS: **BRAYERING**

1. Brayers come in many different sizes.

2. Roll a brayer several times over a multicolored ink pad.

3. After unloading the ink onto the background paper, overstamp and emboss one or several designs in white, or add a photo. Bleaching techniques and stickers also work nicely on these backgrounds.

When brayering with ink, it is especially nice to use a bleached stamping technique, creating a unique focal point.

Add small cut-out shapes to a brayered surface to provide contrast and texture to a card. This card also has a stamped and embossed greeting.

Bristol Board

A stiff, heavy paper whose caliper ranges upward from 0.006 inches.

Brush Marker

A water-based marking pen with a long, broad tip. *See also* Markers.

Burnish

To rub with a tool that causes an especially smooth or polished surface. In paper crafts, a bone folder is most often used for smoothing and burnishing. *See also* Bone Folder.

Button

A fastener made of plastic, metal, or bone often used as an embellishment in card making to add texture or color, or to define corners.

Button cards

The Encyclopedia of Greeting Card Tools & Techniques

CARD SUBMISSION

When an artist or writer sends an original work to a greeting card company with the hopes of selling the work.

CAREER CARD MAKER

An artist or writer (or both) who works primarily for the greeting card industry producing artwork in any media, or the poetry or prose that accompanies the card. *See also* Card Submission.

CARTE-DE-VISITE

A calling or visiting card or a card-backed photograph of a visitor, a celebrity, or a famous place. These cards were popular in the late 1860s.

CEMENT

A PVA glue or acrylic-based adhesive that dries to a raised, clear or opaque finish. These adhesives are used for special effects and their specialty adhering qualities. *See also* Adhesive.

·█ Artist Profile

Kit Allen,
Career Card Maker

After earning his bachelor of fine arts degree from Brigham Young University, Kit Allen was determined to work as an artist, painting first in oils and eventually moving into graphic arts.

librarian.

Following a move to Minnesota, Kit began web-designing and conceived the idea for his first book *Long-johns*. Five years and another move later—this time to Connecticut—the book became reality, and *Longjohns* was published.

Four more children's books followed, and along the way, Great Arrow Graphics published Kit's first greeting cards, and then his "Recycled Greetings" line.

In addition to being a father to five children and a card illustrator, Kit is an art teacher living (for now) in Tomball, Texas. Surrounded by budding artists during the school year, he works intently during the summers on his book projects and card lines.

my guardian angel.

Kit has spent his life on the move, first as part of a military family and then as an adult. Along the way he has created color-filled art that made him smile and opened doors to new friends. He is pleased, knowing he is providing a happy life for his family and still is able to make people smile.

CHALK

Geologically speaking, the chalk used by crafters is actually gypsum, not natural chalk. A sedimentary rock substance, the art material called chalk is ground, pigmented, and then formed and held into shapes using light binders. Chalk is an alkaline substance, versatile and useful for a wide range of paper craft projects and techniques, including shading, highlighting, distressing, and coloring paper.

Chalk comes in a large variety of sizes, shapes, and colors.

Cards made with chalk techniques

HOW-TO BASICS: **CHALKING**

While chalking works on most papers with tooth, embossed papers really showcase the product, highlighting the raised areas with color. Here, blending several analogous colors using a soft applicator, gives the background paper a "watercolory" appearance—a perfect choice for this marker/blender pen focal image.

CHALKBOARD SPRAY PAINT

PRODUCT TIP

Spray several sheets of card stock with chalkboard spray paint. Have it ready for those creative days. Always use spray paints outdoors with plenty of cross ventilation.

CHALKING TOOL

An implement for applying chalk to paper. May include sponges or sponge daubers, cotton swabs, or sponge cosmetics applicators.

CHALKING TIPS

- To prevent smearing, place a piece of computer paper over the majority of the artwork and rest your hand on that, lifting and moving it as necessary.

- A centuries-old artist's tool, the maulstick is a long stick with a cushion on one end that rests on the table surface. It is used to steady the working hand, while keeping it above the artwork. A quick and easy substitute for a maulstick is a ruler.

- It may be necessary to spray a fixative on a finished chalking to prevent smearing.

CHANUKAH CARD

Here are a couple of samples to show you just how creative Chanukah cards can be.

CHARITABLE CONTRIBUTING

A partnership between large non-profit organizations and philanthropic manufacturers and designers, with a percentage of greeting card and product sales benefiting a designated cause or charity.

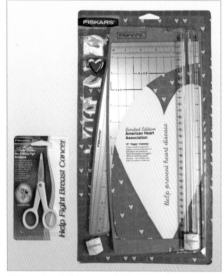

When charitable organizations and philanthropic companies combine their resources, everyone wins.

CHILDREN'S CARD MAKING

Cards made by or with children, using simple tools and materials such as crayons, glitter, rubber stamps and stamp pads, stickers, colored pencils, markers, and glue.

CHRISTMAS CARD

One of the most popular card-sending times of the year is Christmas. With so much to draw from, you can go in many directions when you make your own cards—from personal stories to poignant messages, from humorous anecdotes to hushed reverence. Here are samples to send you on your way. *See also* Holiday Celebration Card.

To make this Christmas card, you use an old credit card to layer a bumpy coat of artist's cement mixed with acrylic paint. Use a popsicle stick to layer on a pattern, such as a tree, snowman or ornament. Sprinkle in a few beads and when dry, mount it inside an aperture card.

Chromolithography

Any lithograph printed in at least three colors. The process was developed in the early 1800s by German printer Alois Senefelder and the term coined in 1837 by Frenchman Godefroy Engelmann. Widely used in the production of Victorian greeting cards, chromolithography produced millions of inexpensive multi-color images, providing affordable greeting cards to the masses.

Clay

Any malleable material able to be molded and fashioned into a dimensional motif. This broad definition includes many types of clay. *See also* Air-Dry Clay and Polymer Clay.

Clear Art Stamp

A tool made from a film negative and hardened liquid polymer, clear stamps provide artists a transparent view for correct image placement. An alternative to the traditional rubber stamp, polymer stamps may yellow or harden over time, especially if exposed to sunlight, indoor lighting, oil-based products, solvent inks, acetone, or bleach. *See also* Stamping.

Clip Art

Ready-made pieces of printed or computerized art. Clip Art can be copied, scanned, or printed from the computer directly onto card stock or paper. It is usually copyright-free, or may have a fee for limited use.

Clip art comes in paper and electronic forms. Use whichever best fits your needs.

COATED PAPER STOCK

Paper with a clay or other coating that may have a glossy, matte, or satin finish. Coated paper generally produces sharp, bright images and intensifies color. *See also* Paper.

Line art and color really pop on glossy stock. The beauty of coated papers is that colors contrast and provide a dimensional appearance, while remaining quite smooth.

Carefully considered, the matte-coated paper is placed behind the glossier sticker paper fans. This contrast in texture is subtle but important and provides added dimension, pushing the colorful background and pulling the fans forward.

COCKLE

The formation of ripples, bubbling, or warped areas in paper. Cockling is caused by uneven moisture uptake or uneven tension during drying, or by excessive humidity.

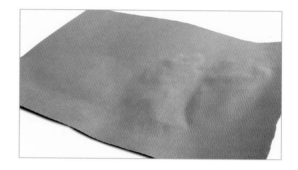

▪▪ HOW-TO BASICS: **PREVENTING COCKLING** ▪▪

- Cockling is a natural occurrence when using dry paper and wet adhesive. It may indicate that something is handmade instead of store-bought.

- To avoid or minimize cockling, use adhesives quickly and sparingly.

- Don't drip, squirt, or scrub adhesives into paper. Instead, put adhesives into a cup and use a brush to apply an even coating, if possible in the opposite direction of the grain.

- Apply adhesive to the back side of the paper first, which will balance the tension caused by the drying and drawing-up.

- Wet the paper completely before adhering it. The paper will dry with an even tension.

COLD-PRESSED PAPER

A variety of paper that has a lightly textured surface, somewhere in between rough and hot-pressed paper. Watercolor artists often prefer it for its ideal absorbency. *See also* Paper.

COLLAGE

An artistic composition made of various materials, such as paper, cloth, or wood, glued onto a surface.

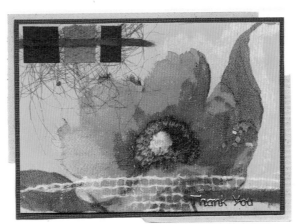

Susan Pickering Rothamel,
Collage Artist

A self-proclaimed pack rat, paper aficionado, and collector of exotic stuff, Susan Pickering Rothamel says, "It's only natural that as a career, I've explored collage and mixed media as my primary form of 'arting.'"

But, when all is said and done, card making is where all the leftover bits come together and satisfy the urge to create—instantly! It is not only great fun, Susan claims, but it's fairly quick to take those leftover "art starts"—the paper-scraps of this and that—add a few fibers or fabric, and then adhere them all to a piece of card, or alter a ready-made greeting card.

Designing your own personal cards is immensely satisfying. It may take a little more time, but the joy of hearing a family member or neighbor say, "We always look forward to seeing what you made this year" makes it worth the investment.

"So," says Susan, "I'll round out Friday and Saturday to plan my cards—deciding on the design for this year's Christmas offerings. On Sunday, I shall ask my brain to rest."

Susan is president of USArtQuest.
www.usartquest.com

The diversity of patterns and colors available in papers today can make anyone's brain go into overdrive. "I marvel at how many things can be made of, covered with, or otherwise embellished with paper. On Monday I can paper-texture a wall, and Tuesday collage a countertop. On Wednesday I can make unique art for the local gallery, and on Thursday fashion my own bathroom accessories. Paper is divinely versatile, becoming whatever you want it to be."

COLOR

A visual experience that can be described as having quantifiable dimensions of hue, saturation, and brightness or lightness. As an element of design, color draws attention, evokes emotions, and conveys messages.

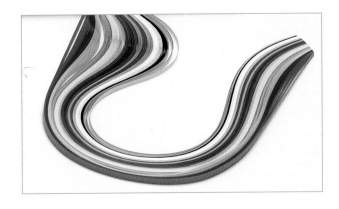

Colors on a card can come from many sources: the paper, the ink, embellishments, and more.

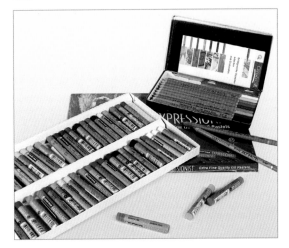

COLOR THEORY TERMS

Analogous Color—Colors adjacent to each other on the color wheel. One color is used as a dominant color, while others are used to enhance the imagery.

Secondary Color—A color formed by mixing equal parts of two primary colors. In art, secondary colors are orange, green, and purple.

Primary Color—Any of three colors from which all others can be made by mixing. In art, primary colors are red, yellow, and blue.

Tertiary Color—A color formed by mixing equal parts of a primary color and a secondary color. Also known as intermediate color.

CONDOLENCE CARD

When you want to express your sympathies, nothing quite touches the heart like a handmade card. Here are a few samples to show you how.

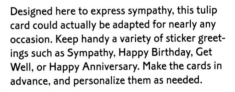

When someone you *love* becomes a *memory* the memory becomes a *Treasure*

Designed here to express sympathy, this tulip card could actually be adapted for nearly any occasion. Keep handy a variety of sticker greetings such as Sympathy, Happy Birthday, Get Well, or Happy Anniversary. Make the cards in advance, and personalize them as needed.

Sympathy

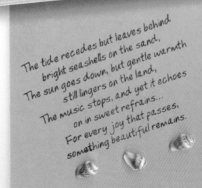

The tide recedes but leaves behind bright seashells on the sand,
The sun goes down, but gentle warmth still lingers on the land,
The music stops, and yet it echoes on in sweet refrains...
For every joy that passes, something beautiful remains.

CONFETTI

Small pieces of colored plastic or paper made to be thrown during a celebratory event. In cardmaking, it may be added to envelopes for a cheerful opening, or glued to a card surface.

CONTRAST

See Color.

COOL COLOR

See Color.

COPYRIGHT

A legal notice that protects "original works of authorship" both published and unpublished, that are expressed in a tangible form, but not the ideas themselves. The symbol for a copyrighted material is ©.

Die-cut letters, all glittery in red, are ideal for this holiday. The confetti adds to the festive nature of the card. Notice, too, how the holly berries repeat the square confetti pattern.

While often just sprinkled into the envelope, confetti is also a great card embellishment. Strategically placed and adhered directly to a fabric flower, it adds a cheerful celebratory touch, without the mess that loose confetti can make.

Corner Edger

Scissors and other devices that cut paper while creating specialty corners or decorative patterns.

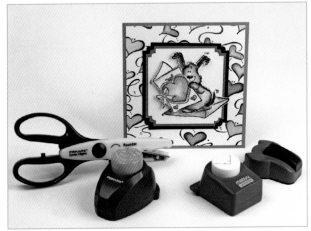

Corner edgers can help you frame your focal point with style.

Simple rounded edges are often as effective as a more fancy corner, especially when placed onto a contrasting sharp-cornered card. In many cases, the adage "less is more" holds true, even in card making.

CORNER PUNCH

A device used to pierce a photograph or paper corner for decorative purposes. *See also* Punch.

CORNER ROUNDER

A punch or scissors used for rounding the corners of photographs and paper. *See also* Corner Edger and Punch.

CORRUGATED PAPER

A heavy paper made to resemble even rows of valleys and mountains. Corrugated papers provide texture and dimension, as well as an opportunity to fill in and embellish the valleys. *See also* Paper.

Add a corrugated section as a way to further embellish a card, using a fine tip adhesive applicator in the paper valleys and some gorgeous microbeads.

CORRUGATOR

A hand tool that ripples paper. Also known as a crimper.

With tools like these, you can create new looks and special effects even with regular paper!

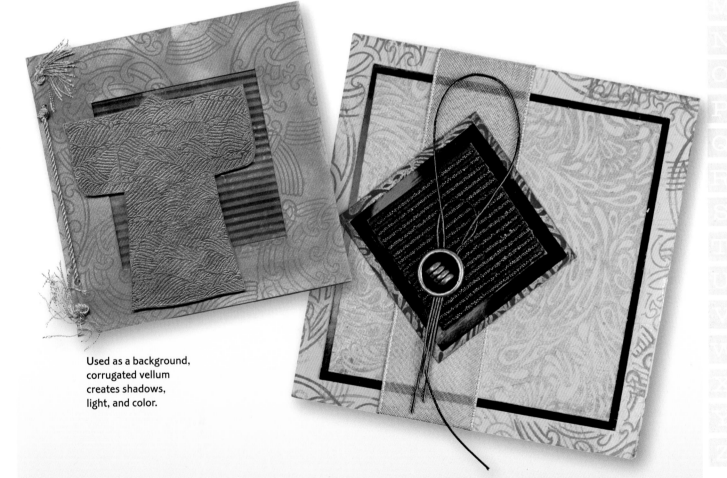

Used as a background, corrugated vellum creates shadows, light, and color.

Corrugated paper adds textural interest to any card, but with the valleys filled with micro-beads, it becomes a much stronger image.

COTTON LINTER

Fibers that adhere to cottonseed after ginning. Cotton linter is used as raw material to produce pulp for cotton papers. It is ideal for making paper castings, decorative accents, and 3-D impressions.

CRACKLE MEDIUM

A medium made to alter the surface of paper or paint by creating fissures, crazing, and crackling, thus giving it an aged appearance.

Crackle medium products

When paste crackle medium is applied, and then aged with glaze, it provides a striking contrast background against the smooth Mica Tile and the colorful fiber and paper layers.

CRAFT KNIFE

A pencil-shaped tool affixed with one of many shaped razor blades attached to one end. Also called artist knives, they are used for lightweight, precise, and intricate cutting, and suitable for cutting most materials used in cardmaking.

Swivel Blade—This is a traditional knife handle containing a small, movable, curved-blade knife, used for intricate cutting. A swivel blade is particularly useful when working with templates as they often have a track for the blade to follow.

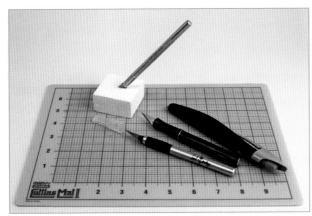

Always use a craft knife on a self-healing cutting mat.

HOW-TO BASICS:
CRAFT KNIFE USE AND SAFETY

- Change the blades often. It is imperative to maintain a sharp blade, held securely in the handle. Dull blades not only make rough cuts, but also slip easier. Paper and cutting surfaces dull blades quickly.

- Do not dispose of stray blades in the trash. Purchase refill blades available in a plastic box, which has a slot for disposing the used blades. Alternatively, wrap the blade in a piece of masking tape or seal inside a scrap of stiff paper.

- Use metal rulers instead of plastic ones because you cannot slice them.

- When using a ruler, hold it firmly in place, but keep fingers clear of the blade.

- Use a safety cap, or store knives with the blade-side down.

- Protect furniture, including glass or plastic laminate. Use a special, self-healing mat for cutting. Or use thick cardboard under your working surface. Wrap a rubber band around the handle of the knife to prevent it from rolling off of the work surface.

CRAZING

The finest lines that occur in a crackle medium or glaze.

CRAYON

A stick of wax mixed with dye or pigment used for coloring a drawing. Wax crayons are simple coloring tools, non-toxic, and available in a huge variety of colors.

Crayola crayons, made by the world's largest manufacturer of crayons, Binney & Smith, are made of petroleum-based paraffin wax. The typical melting point of crayons is 105°F, or 40°C. Swiss-made Caran d'Ache crayons are water-soluble

Draw with crayons and cover the area with plain paper. Press it with a hot iron and reveal exciting and surprising results.

CRAYON RESIST

A technique in which a wax-based crayon and water-based media repel one another. Depending on the paper or crayon used, the repelling of the paint allows the color of the crayon to be highlighted, or to become a highlight.

Used as a resist, crayons produce mixed, but surprising and interesting results. Simply draw or trace a design. Wash over it with watercolors. Use different papers to produce different results. Here glossy card stock actually resists some of the watercolor too.

HOW-TO BASICS:
CRAYON RESIST – VARIATION 1

1. Draw a design or picture with crayons. Light colors work the best.

2. Press hard with the crayons so they will show up under the paint.

3. When complete, lightly brush dark paint over the picture.

4. The areas of crayon will resist the dark paint.

HOW-TO BASICS:
CRAYON RESIST – VARIATION 2

1. Using a glossy card stock, stamp an image in black or other dark ink.

2. Color an area to highlight with a white crayon.

3. Sponge inks to cover the entire card.

4. Use a paper towel to remove ink from the crayoned area.

OTHER CRAYON RESIST THEMES

- Antique metallic crayoning, using black or dark tempera paints.

- Crackle finish the paper by crumpling a completely crayoned paper, then cover with paint.

- Try various colors to produce different effects.

- For rainbow effects, cover the entire surface of the paper with various colors, and then apply a thick water-based paint. When it's dry, scrape off the paint in specific areas.

CRIMPER

A tool used to corrugate paper or card stock. *See also* Corrugator.

CROP

To trim the edges of an image, often to improve its composition.

This faux lace background paper made using ATG and mica flakes appears more finished, as well as balanced, when cropped and framed with a narrow frame of colored card stock.

CROP MARK

A line or mark indicating where the pages or photographs will be trimmed.

CUTTING MAT

See Self-Healing Cutting Mat.

CYANOACRYLATE

An extremely fast-cure adhesive available in various thicknesses and cure times. Cyanoacrylate adhesives may yellow or become brittle over time and should have limited use, adhering only the most difficult nonporous surfaces and polymer clay. *See also* Adhesives.

DEBOSSING

A technique in which paper areas recess, or go down, rather than rise up. *See also* Emboss.

DECKLE EDGE

A deckle edge can be defined as:

1. The naturally rough or feathered edge of untrimmed handmade paper. 2. A type of feathered edge imitated in commercial papers. 3. Hand-cut paper edges created using special scissors, cutters, or rulers to resemble untrimmed handmade papers.

HOW-TO BASICS: DECKLED FOCAL POINT

1. Deckling is not just used for paper edges, but also for the focal point itself. Select a soft fibered paper, and use a pre-formed hard shape as a template.

2. Follow along the edge with a water-loaded brush.

3. Gently tear along the wet area using your fingers.

4. When dry, mount the deckle-edged heart shape onto crisp, cut card stock.

Begin with the direct-to-paper technique on glossy card stock and then die cut the flowers. Layer each flower individually with their separately cut centers, and then slightly bend the petals to give them dimension.

Not just die cut, these fish have also been embossed. The embossing is highlighted with ink. Beautiful Asian papers and embellishments accentuate the authentic chopsticks, which are being given as the gift itself.

This charming tri-fold card displays fanciful embossed flowers, colorfully chalked and scattered onto bright pink borders.

Digital Image

An image obtained by electronic data and storage rather than by the chemical processes in traditional photography. Obtained by using digital cameras, camcorders, scanners, or other devices, digital imagery captures and stores pictures without film. When printed, the images are considered color photographs.

Dimensional Adhesive

A PVA or acrylic-based adhesive that dries to raised, clear glass-like or a raised opaque finish. These adhesives are used for special effects and for their specialty adhering qualities. *See also* Adhesive.

Card with digital image

DIMENSIONAL EMBOSSING

The use of stencils and relief products, such as clay, artist cements, and pastes, to bring added depth to a raised or lowered image or word(s). Also known as Relief Embossing and Dimensional Stenciling. *See also* Emboss.

HOW-TO BASICS:
DIMENSIONAL EMBOSSING

1. Spread the cement evenly and in one swipe, if possible, through a plastic or brass stencil.

2. Immediately clean the stencil with water. While the cement is still wet, sprinkle on bits of mica, glitter, or other small particles. When the design is completely covered, allow it to dry thoroughly.

Begin by color blocking with inks, and then apply the dimensionally stenciled design. When it's complete, color the design with pearlescent paint.

After stenciling the design and allowing it to dry thoroughly, use various inks on the surface to create the stained glass effect.

Use several different stencils to create a sampler piece. When the cement is dry, gild the entire area, bringing a continuity and sophistication of design.

DIRECT TO PAPER

A technique of moving ink or paint from one place to another, either by using the inkpad or other sponge-like device, directly onto card stock.

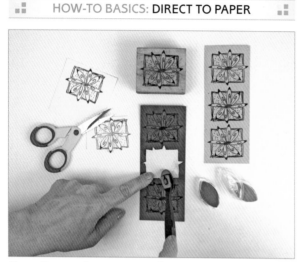

Stamp the same image onto small scraps of paper and cut them out. Stamp and emboss the images onto card stock. Use the scraps as a mask, fitting them over the card stock images and begin using ink pads to smooth ink color over the background. When the scrap is removed, the stamped areas can be colored in separately, using markers, ink, chalks, or sparkling watercolors.

DISTRESSED PAPER

A piece of paper that has been transformed into an older-looking version of itself by wrinkling, folding, wetting, sanding, or otherwise damaging the sheet.

DOUBLE MOUNT

An art or photo framing technique using two papers, each progressively larger than the original focal point.

DOMINO

A game piece, altered and used as a card embellishment or focal point.

Collage a pattern directly onto a domino and mount it as the focal point on a color-blocked greeting card.

The colors and textures of the handmade paper feature pretty deckle edging. The leaf imagery is stronger after double-mounting than it would be mounted directly to the card made from a plain brown paper bag.

Dry Adhesive

Any adhesive that does not require the evaporation of a liquid to hold fast one element to another. *See also* Adhesive and Tape.

Dry Brushing

The technique of filling a brush with paint, removing virtually all of it, and then brushing the nearly dry brush across paper to alter and subdue color, or to enhance protrusions, wrinkles, and paper-embossed areas.

Dry Embossing

To impress an image into paper using pressure and a brass or plastic stencil and paper, or thin metal, achieving a subtle raised or relief surface. *See also* Emboss.

Materials
Light box or window
Stylus, double-ended
Removable/repositionable tape
Embossing template (metal or plastic)
Paper or thin metal sheeting

Instructions
1. Tape a stencil onto a window or light box.

2. Position paper over the stencil, securing it with removable tape.

3. Firmly but gently press the paper into the stencil, moving a stylus only around the edges of the design.

4. Use the larger end of the stylus for more open areas, and the smaller end for the detail areas.

Dry embossing can be mechanically reproduced. This background paper is a good example, although it could just as easily have been hand-embossed, too!

The Encyclopedia of Greeting Card Tools & Techniques

TIPS FOR DRY EMBOSSING

- Rub the paper with waxed paper so the stylus will glide smoothly.

- A heavier paper will give a more finished effect.

- There is no right or wrong side to a stencil, except with letters and numbers. Simply turn a stencil over to get a mirror image.

- Use the largest stylus possible for the stencil opening. The smaller the stylus, the greater the possibility of tearing the paper.

- Gently, but firmly, trace the edge of the open design.

- Store stencils separately in bags, envelopes, photo pockets, or a handmade stencil book.

- Add color to a stenciled design using dry powdered pigments, chalk, acrylics, or pastels working in thin glazes or layers of color.

DRY MOUNT

Pasting with heat-sensitive adhesives.

DUMMY

A preliminary layout showing the position of illustrations and text as they are to appear in the final reproduction.

DVD/CD COVER

Used in creative card making as the card itself or as the "envelope" to hold a card. Also known as jewel case. To prevent breakage when mailing, place the cover in a padded envelope.

DYE

A water- or solvent-soluble substance made to color ink, paper, and textiles. Dye colors are less stable over a long period than pigment colors; however, when applied and protected properly, they have a relatively long life and allow a greater color variety.

Dry embossing onto soft Indian papers produces lovely, crisp, stenciled designs.

E-CARD

A greeting card chosen and sent via the Internet. E-cards may be traditional in style or personalized, and they may include music and moving components (animation).

EASTER CARD

Although it's not generally a holiday many people associate with card-giving, Easter can inspire you to produce very creative cards. There are two sides to Easter: the religious and the juvenile. Here are some samples that reflect both. *See also* Holiday Celebration Card.

Happy Easter

With Love

Believe

ELEMENT

As the word pertains to paper crafting: any photograph, embellishment, color, paper layer, or design shape used within a card's composition.

EMBELLISHMENT

Any slightly or fully dimensional decorative element that enhances a card.

Beads, buttons, cabochons, words, and other objects can all become embellishments on a greeting card. Don't be shy—experiment!

A simply stamped butterfly becomes dazzling when rhinestones are added. Add even more sparkle using double-sided tape and Mica D'Lights.

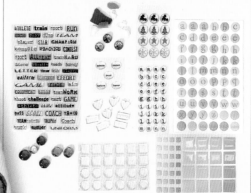

Grace Taormina,
Embellishments

Grace Taormina's love for creating has led her on an interesting and varied career path. She has designed and imported women's apparel, worked in sales and marketing in the gift industry, and labored as a teacher and product designer in the art and craft industry, serving as the "go-to" designer for Rubber Stampede and Delta Creative.

Grace has explored the creative potential of rubber-stamp art in her books *The Complete Guide to Rubber Stamping* and *The Complete Guide to Decorative Stamping*, as well as in many popular magazines and in guest appearances on the *Carol Duvall Show* and *Decorating with Style*.

She lives near San Francisco and says, "Even with all I have done, I most enjoy teaching others the joy of embellishing their art and life with creativity."

Shadow stamping provides a colorful background to the silhouette stamped image. Use a ribbon to enhance the one-third composition rule. The dragonfly is not only an appropriate embellishment for the subject matter, but it also draws the eye into the composition and ties the layers together.

93

EMBOSS

To create a raised or lowered image or word by using one of several methods, including pressure, heat, or resins. *See also* Blind Embossing, Dimensional Embossing, Dry Embossing, and Heat Embossing.

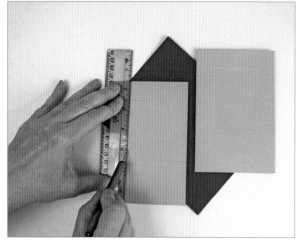

Creating a blind embossed raised edge gives the appearance of another paper layer, or even a frame for the artwork or focal point.

EMBOSSED PAPER

Paper that has been machine- or hand-embossed.

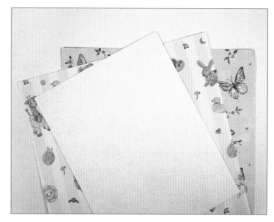

Embossed paper makes a wonderful background—as well as producing exceptional highlights—for your greeting cards.

Embossed paper looks spectacular when aged with chalks or inks, highlighted with oil crayons, or just kissed with mica-based watercolors on the raised patterning.

Standard Envelope—Envelopes differ by size and flap type, are made with or without windows, and standardization differs by country. Envelopes used in the U.S. (also known as Standard), and ISO metric system (used throughout Europe and many other countries) are available in every possible size and configuration.

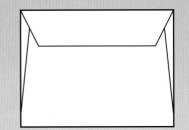

Announcement
You can use these, with either a pointed or flat flap, for most greeting cards.

#	Size
A-2	4⅜ x 5¾ inches
A-4	4¾ x 6½ inches
A-7	5¼ x 7¼ inches
A-8	5½ x 8⅛ inches
A-10	6¼ x 9⅝ inches
Slim	3⅞ x 8⅞ inches

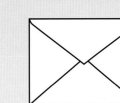

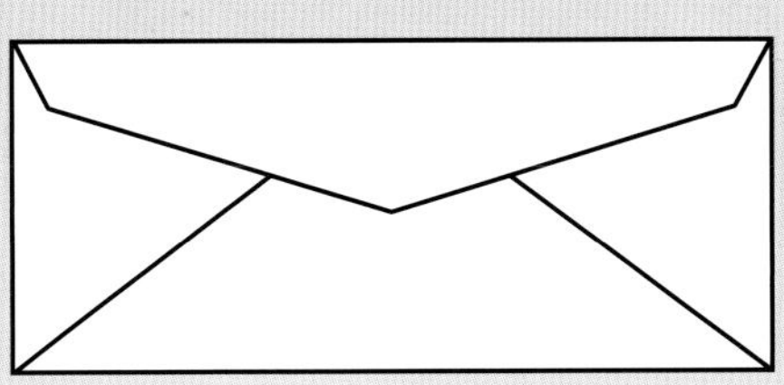

Business or Commercial
You can use these for long, narrow greeting cards

#	Size
6¼	3½ x 6 inches
6¾	3⅝ x 6½ inches
7¾	3⅞ x 7½ inches
8	3⅞ x 7½ inches
8⅝	3⅝ x 8⅝ inches
9	3⅞ x 8⅞ inches
10	4⅛ x 9½ inches
11	4½ x 10⅜ inches
12	4¾ x 11 inches
14	5 x 11½ inches

Baronial (Invitation)
You can use these for smaller greeting cards, invitations, or as inner envelopes.

#	Size
2	3³⁄₁₆ x 4¼ inches
4	3⅝ x 4⅝ inches
5	4⅛ x 5⅛ inches
5¼	4¼ x 5¼ inches
5½	4⅜ x 5⅝ inches
5¾	4½ x 5¾ inches
6	5 x 6 inches

ISO Envelope Standards—These are C-series envelopes designed to accommodate ISO A paper sizes. For example, a C5 envelope accommodates an A5 sheet flat or an A4 folded once. The sizes are provided in millimeters and in inches (for reference).

Type	Size (mm / inches)	Comments
C3	324 x 458 / 12¾ x 18	A3 sheet (uncommon)
B4	250 x 353 / 9⅞ x 13⅞	C4 envelope
C4	229 x 324 / 9 x 12¾	A4 sheet (common)
B5	176 x 250 / 7 x 9⅞	C5 envelope
C5	162 x 229 / 6⅜ x 9	A4 sheet folded once = A5 (common)
B6	125 x 176 / 5 x 7	A4 sheet folded in ¼ (common)
C6	114 x 162 / 4½ x 6⅜	A4 sheet folded in ¼ (common)
DL	110 x 220 / 4¼ x 8¾	A4 sheet folded in ⅓
C6/C5	114 x 229 / 4½ x 9	A4 sheet folded in ⅓ (common)
C7/6	81 x 162 / 3¼ x 6⅜	A5 sheet folded in ⅓ (common)
C7	81 x 114 / 3¼ x 4½	A5 sheet folded in ¼ (common)

TIPS FOR ADDRESSING ENVELOPES

- Write legibly, so as not to confuse the optical reading equipment.

- Always use the ZIP/postal code.

- When using software to print addresses, always print the barcodes whenever possible.

- Use simple fonts, such as Arial or Helvetica, and a font size over 12 points.

- Avoid using any graphics in the address zone, as it may confuse the optical reader.

- For formal address, write titles on the envelope, such as "Mr. John Smith" or "Mr. and Mrs. John Smith." Less formally, write "John Smith" or "John and Mary Smith."

- With professionals, use "Dr. and Mrs. John Smith," not "John Smith, M.D., and Mrs. Smith."

- If both the husband and the wife are doctors: "The Doctors Smith."

- If one spouse is a doctor and the other is not: "Mr. John Smith and Dr. Mary Smith."

- When military rank is an issue, the higher rank comes before the lower rank, such as "Major Louise Stover and Lieutenant John Stover."

- If a couple is not married but shares an address, use two lines. Do not add an "and":
    Ms. Hattie Curtis
    Mr. Arthur DeMar

- Otherwise, try to get the addressee's name all on one line. When the husband has an unusually long name, indent the wife's title and name on a second line:
    The Honorable James Henry Churchill and
        Mrs. James Churchill

EPHEMERA

Printed items produced with the intent of conveying content of some importance to an era, but which are then discarded or recycled. Ephemera can include newspapers, magazines, cigar wrappers, fruit crate labels, ticket stubs, match covers, invitations, pages from books—nearly anything printed, including greeting cards themselves. "Ephemera" is from the Greek word meaning "that which lasts but for a day."

A plethora of ephemera

A pretty floral party napkin holds just the right memories and is the perfect paper ephemera to use when making and sending your hostesses thank you cards.

ETIQUETTE

Practices, rules, and manners to help others feel comfortable. Greeting card rules of etiquette are simple, yet when followed provide a sense of style and tradition.

TIPS

- The proper way to place a card into an envelope is to insert the folded side first and the design face-up, toward the flap.
- If your family creates a holiday newsletter, send it only to family and friends.
- Greeting cards for family and friends may be casual in appearance, but for business, even when handmade, they should have a more professional appearance.
- Send a card to everyone who sends you one.
- Thank-you cards should be sent within one to two weeks after you receive the gift.
- Always include your return address on the envelope.
- Hand-writing an envelope is more personal, and preferable, to using computerized address labels.
- Give children special pens and stickers to decorate their envelopes.
- Check your spelling.
- Sending e-cards is an immediate way to say thanks; however, they should still be followed up with a hand-written card or note.
- E-mailed greeting cards are not a substitute for actual holiday cards.

EYELET

A metal, plastic, or rubber ring or grommet that, when inserted into a hole and flattened, reinforces the hole. Also used as decorative accents in card making, eyelets come in dozens of styles and colors.

EYELET SETTER

A tool for fastening eyelets.

HOW-TO BASICS: EYELET SETTING

1. Begin by punching a hole into your card, using a hole punch the same size or slightly smaller than the desired eyelet.

2. Set the eyelet into the hole and turn the card over. From the backside, set the eyelet setter onto the small aperture and tap the end of the setter with a hammer. Continue tapping until the eyelet is flattened into a rounded circle.

FABRIC

A textural alternative to paper in card making.

Mesh fabric pillows, easily stitched by hand or machine, give cards a real handmade touch, encapsulating personal messages or objects inside.

This card uses metallic hot glue and fabric eyes. It may look like a simple card; however, the composition is quite complex, striking a balance between whimsy and modern design.

FADE PROOF OR FADE RESISTANT

A color that does not fade or resists change when stored away from a light source or other environmental factors.

FAN FOLD

A paper fold that resembles a traditional fan or accordion. When complete, it is narrower at the bottom than it is at the top. *See also* Accordion Folding.

A three-dimensional fan fold card

FASTENER

Any device used to attach two or more card components. Fasteners are often used as decorative accents, having no other function than an aesthetic element.

Pretty ribbon tightly placed across corners performs as well as any hardware-like fastener. Firmly attach it under the artwork, and slip in the two corners.

There are many, many fasteners to choose from. Find the one that's right for the card you're making.

Decorative brads come in hundreds of designs and not only provide a fastening device, but also cute embellishments.

Vinyl hinges are a terrific alternative to using actual metal hardware. This particular card opens on the bottom portion only.

Mica tiles are easily punched using a hand punch or screw punch, providing an opportunity to use a myriad of fastener types.

FATHER'S DAY CARD

A card sent to your father, grandfather, stepfather, and father figure. Here are a couple of samples to inspire you to create your own. *See also* Holiday Celebration Card.

A paper-folded (origami) collar and tie, adhered to a decorative but more masculine card stock, looks just like a plaid shirt any dad would be proud to wear!

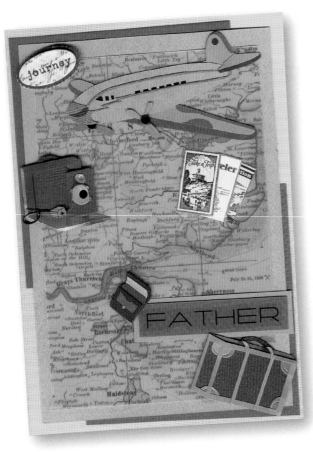

FIBER

A textile material, such as modern yarn and embroidery threads, that is a trendy technique for decorating paper and card stock.

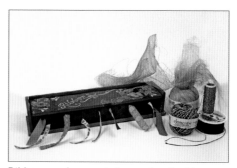

Ribbon, mesh, yarn, twine, and embroidery floss—just some of the fibers you can incorporate into a greeting card.

BE
WITH
THOSE
WHO
HELP
YOUR
BEING

Frankie Fioretti,
Fiber Arts

Frankie Fioretti's card making methods exhibit a self-assured sense of balance and design, even when created somewhat serendipitously. "If it means combining color with texture, I'll try or mix almost anything," she says.

Through rubber stamping, she began working with Penny Black Rubberstamps and USArtQuest, Inc., designing cards and paper, as well as producing professional samples for catalogues.

Her advice for card makers is to leave the inside of cards blank until it's time to send them. "Doing so makes nearly any well-designed card automatically suited to a recipient or to the occasion."

Frankie explores the wonderful world of surface design, while teaching creativity and encouraging others to follow her love of playing with and investigating art materials through card making.

Frankie has been in the "creative industry" for more than 30 years. Her journey began as a quilter, which led her to rubber stamps as a means to adapt her own textile designs for quilting.

FILM ADHESIVE

See Dry Adhesive.

FINDINGS

Fasteners and construction components used in jewelry making.

FINISH

The condition of a paper surface. A high finish refers to a smooth, hard surface. A low finish refers to a relatively rough, toothy surface.

FIXATIVE

A substance, usually an aerosol spray, that aids in preventing fading or smudging of art materials such as chalks, pastels, and pencil.

Not all fixatives are the same. Read the can before you buy.

FLIP CARD

Any card in which a decorative part of the card can turn, fold, or flip, revealing both sides.

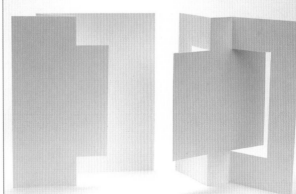

Starting with a simple template, you can fashion some truly creative cards.

Flip card

FLITTER

A mass-production process in which glitter is affixed to produce an iridescent or multi-colored sparkling effect.

FLOWER

Any dry, pressed, preserved paper, silk, or plastic leaves and flowers in card making.

Flowers and leaves can be purchased or pressed and stored inside old telephone books. The Microfleur offers a fast way to preserve summer flowers for instant use.

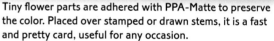

Tiny flower parts are adhered with PPA-Matte to preserve the color. Placed over stamped or drawn stems, it is a fast and pretty card, useful for any occasion.

While not technically a flower, this pressed skeletonized leaf provides the autumnal feeling needed for this colorful card. The acrylic painted background was sprayed with webbing spray, unifying the multi-colored background.

If I had a single flower for every time I think about you, I could walk forever in my garden.

Claudia Ghandi

Flush

Typeset copy that is vertically aligned at the left or right margin.

Foam Stamp

A foam image adhered to a foam block, this stamp is ideal for fabric stamping and stamping bolder images on textured paper. Foam stamp designs have a more graphic, less detailed look. Foam stamps generally are much less expensive than wood-handled stamps. *See also* Stamping.

Foam stamps provide a certain look that translates well on a greeting card.

Foil

A metallic, plastic-like material applied to paper using a heat-set method, hot stamping, or with adhesives using pressure. Foil comes in rolls or sheets and a multitude of colors.

Foiling

The art of applying foil to paper or card stock to form words, lines, patterns, borders, or to enhance imagery.

Just as easy as foil tape, shiny rub-on foil is applied to dry tacky Duo adhesive or double-sided tape. After burnishing it down, leaving the edges less than perfect, add layers of paper and a focal point.

Adhesive-backed foil tape is simple to apply and imparts a metallic frame feature for a strong focal image.

FOLD-OUT CARD

Any card that can be manipulated by exhibiting one, two, or multiple folds. You can even fold these cards into unusual patterns so that they have cut-out or pop-up sections. *See also* Accordion Folding.

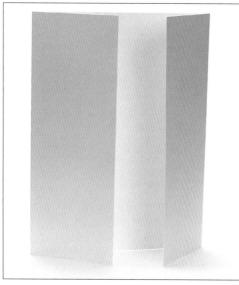

The gate fold template provides a foundation for some fun cards for both children and adults.

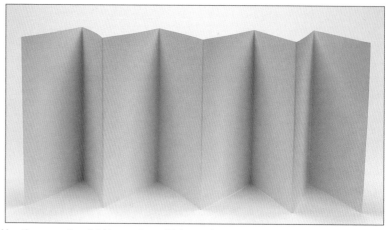

Use the accordion fold to create multi-layered, multi-faceted cards.

The shadow box fold requires a little patience, but it can pay off in screams of delight.

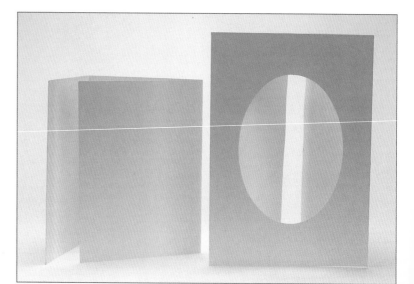

Two tri-fold card patterns, one with a cut-out frame and one without

may sunshine
and flowers
brighten
your day

hello

Get We Soon.

Gilding

The art of applying gold, silver, or other metal leaf to a surface.

Gilding comes in many colors including gold, silver, copper, and beautiful metallic variegated colors.

1. Stamp using gilding adhesive and sponge. When dry, add gilding or glistening metallic pigment.

2. Sponges with varying textures can be used to produce droplet effects. Use gilding adhesive and when dry, add gilding or pigment.

3. Paint on gilding adhesive, as you would watercolor. When dry, add gilding.

4. Create a faux lace using Great Tape. Apply and then nearly rub off the tape. Apply gilding and pigment for a unique bordering or embellishing technique.

5. Add a few drops of leafing adhesive to a Fine Liner, and you've got a great way to write with adhesive. It's gorgeous when gilded with pigments or leafing. Be sure to wash the tool well with liquid soap and water.

GLASSINE

A paper product that is resistant to oil, air, and water. Paper fibers are pressed into molds, allowed to dry in sheets, and then pressed through hot rollers, which makes the fibers lie flat and in the same direction. The result is a very smooth paper product. While nearly transparent, the pulp also may be dyed or made opaque with additives.

Glassine envelopes

GLITTER

Bits of shiny particles used for decorating cards. Apply glitter using various glues or tapes to most surfaces.

Glitter products are easy and fun to use, and the results speak for themselves.

HOW-TO BASICS:
APPLYING GLITTER TO CARDS

1. Stamp or print an image.

2. Black ink provides a high contrast between the glitter and the design itself.

3. Use a touch of watercolor pencil to shade the ornament.

4. Carefully brush a fluid adhesive onto some of the design areas.

5. While wet, sprinkle on one color of glitter.

6. Always do one color at a time, completing it before going onto the next color.

Cards with glitter

GLUE STICK

A round stick of solid glue used to adhere paper to paper. Glue sticks are extremely easy to use; however, as an adhesive for paper crafts, they have a relatively short adhering life expectancy. *See also* Adhesive.

GOUACHE WATERCOLOR

Opaque watercolor containing a colored pigment with a gum binder and an opaque filler. *See also* Watercolor.

GRADUATION CARD

When a friend or loved one graduates, whether it's from a prestigious university or from kindergarten, send a little handmade card to let them know it's a special day. Here are some samples to help get you started. *See also* Special Occasion Card.

The beauty of watercolor is that it can be done nearly any time or any place with few materials. This small study was painted as a tribute to the artist Charles Reid.

GRAIN

The direction in which most fibers in paper run, as a result of the papermaking process. Paper tears more easily with the grain than against it. For some paper varieties, folds made parallel to the grain cause less damage and create smoother, less bulky folds.

GREETING CARD ASSOCIATION

The trade organization representing greeting card and stationery publishers, as well as allied members of the industry. Formed in the U.S. in 1941 in response to a War Department order during World War II to reduce paper use by 25 percent, the Greeting Card Association has evolved over the years since. In 1988, it initiated the Louie awards to celebrate creative excellence in the industry.

GUIDELINES FOR SUBMITTING CARDS

See Card Submission.

GUM ARABIC

A water-soluble gum obtained from the acacia tree and used in lithographic processes. Also, an acid-free powder or liquid binder used to make watercolors.

Two brands of gum arabic

H

HALLOWEEN CARD

Halloween is usually a hands-on holiday—escorting the little ones door-to-door or passing out treats to the witches and ghosts who ring your bell—but why not make an extra special treat by sending out a handmade card to those you know will appreciate it. Here are a few samples to show you how. *See also* Holiday Celebration Card.

Halo and Loop

A method of mounting stamps that uses hook-and-loop tape to attach the polymer or rubber to an acrylic block. This method allows for more accurate placement when stamping.

Hand-Carved Stamp

A tool or material, cut by hand, that produces an image over and over again. *See also* Stamping.

HOW-TO BASICS:
MAKING STAMPS

1. On an easy-to-obtain large, white eraser, draw a design with a ball point pen.
2. Color in the low and in-between-the-design areas.
3. Carefully cut away the little background bits, using a craft knife or carving tool.
4. Ink the design and stamp away!

Handmade Paper

Paper that is not machine-made. It is usually textural, often containing bits of fiber, mica, glitter, or confetti. *See also* Paper.

Hard Pastel

A stick of color, which contains a higher percentage of pigment to binder, providing a firmer more defined drawing texture and detail. *See also* Pastel.

Hardware

Any metal or plastic embellishment or attaching device used to join two or more items or to decorate the card surface when card making. *See also* Found Object.

If it's made of metal or plastic and you can use it on a greeting card, it's hardware.

HEAT EMBOSSING

A technique that uses a stamped image or tool, ink or gilding adhesive, thermal embossing powder, and heating tool to create a raised image when heat is applied. Also known as thermal embossing. *See also* Emboss, Embossing Powder, and Thermography.

HEAT TOOL

A tool designed to heat embossing powder to a temperature at which it becomes liquid and smooth. The tool can reach a temperature of nearly 700°F, so care must be taken to protect paper or work surfaces. Heat tool holders are a nice addition to a studio, as they also perform as a "third hand," holding the tool firmly in place while it is on or off.

A typical heat-embossing tool and stand

HOLE PUNCH

A mechanical tool that makes a hole in paper. Older devices simply made circular holes and were most often used as an office tool. Craft manufacturers now make devices that will punch decorative shapes so that the holes themselves become the decorative embellishments. *See also* Punch.

HOLIDAY CELEBRATION CARD

A purchased or handmade card given as a remembrance or to celebrate a holiday. (For a listing of U.S. and international holidays, see page 274.) *See also* Chanukah Card, Christmas Card, Easter Card, Father's Day Card, Halloween Card, Independence Day Card, Kwanzaa Card, Mother's Day Card, New Year's Card, St. Patrick's Day Card, Thanksgiving Card, and Valentine's Day Card.

After stamping with permanent ink onto the Mica Tile, a light coat of gilding adhesive was added to each section. When dry, adding section by section, use various colors of leafing. A rub-on tag completes this more masculine-looking card.

Die-cut metal greetings may be purchased in a specific color, or painted to match the color scheme of any card. Here, the complementary colors of red and green are further enhanced with spots of ivory and tan, providing a clean, crisp look to this card.

Recycling old holiday cards is just smart cardmaking! From the original card, three smaller cards were made. This one included the snowman and deer, which looks so festive when placed on the bright red background, and surrounded by a complementary colored paper.

Hot Glue

An adhesive that is applied in a liquid form while hot, and adheres and hardens as it cools. *See also* Adhesive.

Use a hot glue gun like a paintbrush, dispensing hot liquid glue into interesting abstract or representative drawings. Just before it cools completely, carefully place flat pieces of gilding or dust on mica pigments. When completely cool, use a textured sponge to remove any extra particles.

Hot-Pressed Paper

A smooth, glazed paper surface produced by rolling and pressing a finished sheet of paper through hot metal cylinders. *See also* Paper.

Huffing

Exhaling on an inked stamp image to keep it moist before stamping. This process can extend the ink to allow a second impression without re-inking.

INK

A fluid, semi-fluid, gel, or paste containing pigments or dyes used in pens, brushes, and pads for drawing, writing, stamping, and printing. Ink for each of these purposes has its own composition and physical property.

A sampling of inks

INKJET PRINTING

A process in which an image or text is transferred to paper or fabric by depositing small ink droplets onto the surface.

INKJET TRANSFER PAPER

A special paper that you can print onto using a computer and inkjet printer. You can then turn over the paper and iron the image onto card stock.

This fold-out card says "Thanks" in a big way. Using both watercolor ink and rubberstamp inks on glossy stock pops the color.

Use alcohol-based inks on glossy cardstock or the reverse side of clear acetate. Stamp an image and then sprinkle it with sparkling embossing powder, glitter, or flitter.

INK PAD

A clear or colored ink-soaked pad used to wet the stamp, then the paper. *See also* Stamping.

INTERFERENCE

Paint or pigment that contains mica particles combined with pigment or dye to achieve an overall iridescent, pearlescent, or metallic appearance. *See also* Mica.

INTERFERENCE MICA

Tiny, transparent mica flakes, coated on all sides with a thin layer of metal oxide—either iron oxide or titanium dioxide—that is highly refractive and reflective simultaneously. The thickness of the metal oxide layer determines the size of the light wavelength, which determines the color of the iridescence. The pearlescent quality when used as a watercolor is particularly brilliant on a dark background. *See also* Mica.

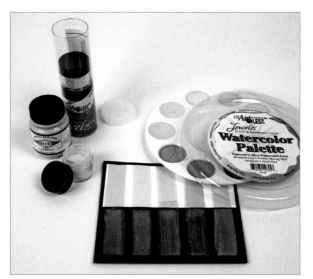

Paint with interference mica as you would with watercolors.

Interference colors show their truest iridescence when applied to dark cardstocks. For easy cards, simply stamp, emboss, and paint. Making beautiful cards has never been so easy.

Apply peel-off gold stickers to card stock, using both the positive and negative shapes. Fill in the areas using the interference watercolors. Cut and assemble each square to resemble a mosaic tile floor.

Using interference watercolor paints with watercolor markers enlarges the color choices for card makers. It is also a terrific way to learn about shading and color. The markers and watercolors will work on any dark or light surface.

INVITATION

A card that invites the recipient to an event or special occasion. A close cousin to the greeting card, an invitation should match the style of the event. *See also* Invitation Card.

INVITATION TIPS

- Always include the following:
  - Name of the host or hostess
  - Purpose of the invitation (birthday party, wedding, holiday, etc.) or name of the person to be honored
  - Day, date, and time of the event
  - Location of the event (street address, city and state, but no ZIP code)
  - Appropriate attire
- Proofread your invitation for mistakes and forgotten information.
- Formal invitations require eight weeks' advance notice.
- Try to send out informal invitations at least four weeks in advance.

This quilled invitation to a bridal shower is both personalized and a forever keepsake.

INVITATION

You can't throw a party without invitations, and your guests are sure to come when you send them a card you made yourself. Here are some creative samples to help get you started.

IRIS FOLDING

The art of folding, then layering paper to form patterns resembling the iris of the human eye.

Joyce Haefke,
Iris Folding

Joyce Haefke loves paper and paper art of all kinds. "From rubber stamping to scrapbooking, as well as art journals, bookmaking, collage, assemblage, and quilling, I love the process of working with paper," she says.

"But, iris folding," she continues, "ah, well, that's actually what started all of this!"

One day, Joyce began experimenting with iris folding. That led her to develop unique paper-folding patterns, and then paper-folding kits and materials. Dreamer's Designs was a natural evolution, and Joyce, whose samples are finely finished and highly detailed, now wows even experienced paper crafters in classes and at consumer shows.

"My favorite part of all of this, though," she says, "is the sense of satisfaction one gets when working out a pattern, introducing it to other card makers, and then seeing them so happy with the resulting cards they've made themselves."

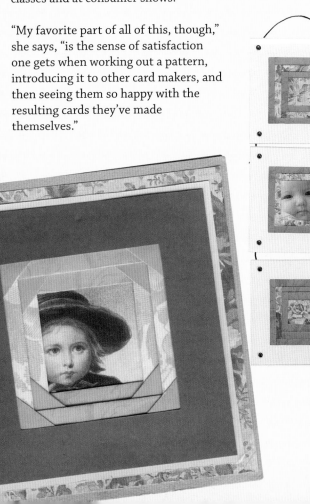

JEWELRY

An adornment or ornament on a greeting card, jewelry can be made of nearly any material including plastic, glass, metal, paper, or found objects. Jewelry can add depth, substance, and fun to any card.

Jewelry—if you think it looks good now, wait until you put it on a card designed specifically for it!

Dee Gruenig's designs are always colorful, and lamination shows her color choices off best. The golf bag and hanging charms, made into a pin, not only produce a memorable card, but a fun gift.

JUSTIFY

To space out lines of type so that both left and right margins are flush. Since the message of a greeting card is often its most important attribute, don't let the text you write (or copy) be lost in a scrawl.

These cards show how to attach laminated pins to the card, and keep them in place during mailing. Simply place a small piece of paper-covered cardstock between the pinback and card, filling the space, which also helps prevent the pinback from being crushed.

KALEIDOSCOPE CARD

A card with optical patterns similar to those derived from the shifting and colorful visuals made by a kaleidoscope. These cards are often created from photographs, stamping techniques, or colored patterned papers. *See also* Card Making.

HOW-TO BASICS:
MAKING KALEIDOSCOPE CARDS

Follow each step as shown below, using a bone folder. Continue until you've completed the pinwheel. Each pinwheel takes eight completely folded pieces.

magenta stamp copied onto copy ppr to make folding tiles

1. Begin by stamping or making a pattern, using lightweight card stock.

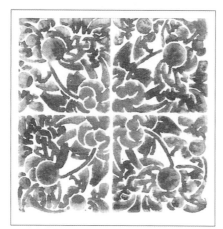

2. Stamp the same design eight times. To make more than one of these cards, color copy the original eight times and cut each on the outside edge.

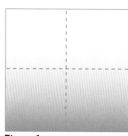

Figure 1

3. With the pattern side up, fold the card stock both horizontally and vertically, as shown in figure 1. The pattern will be on the inside.

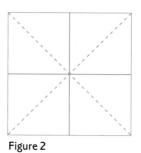

Figure 2

4. With the pattern side down, fold the card stock from corner to corner, as shown in figure 2. The pattern will be on the outside.

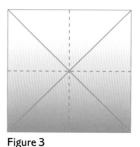

Figure 3

5. With the pattern side up, pinch-in on the blue lines, as shown in figure 3.

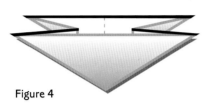

Figure 4

6. With the pattern on the outside, pinch the triangle to flatten it, as shown in figure 4.

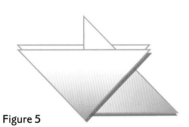

Figure 5

7. With the pattern to the outside, assemble the pieces, gluing or taping them on the backside.

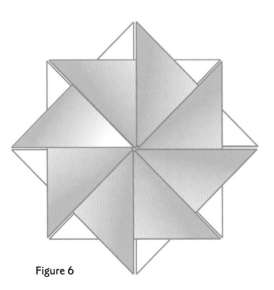

Figure 6

8. Assemble all eight pieces, as shown in figure 6. The last piece just "wiggles" in.

9. Adhere the finished pinwheel to a patterned background paper to complete your card.

While you can make your own papers, as shown in the first card sample, specialty papers are available for this technique. They are both easy and colorful. All that you need to do is cut the papers and assemble the kaleidoscope.

KINETIC CARD

A card that exhibits a movement or motion from one or more elements attached to the card. *See also* Moveable Card.

KROMECOAT

A brand of cover-weight, glossy paper, double coated on one side of the paper. It is ideal for stamping, giving a crisp look to stamped images. A spray sealer or embossing powder will keep pigment inks from smearing.

KWANZAA CARD

Kwanzaa is a time to remember, so show your friends you remember them by sending a handmade card. See the samples here to get your creative juices flowing.

Small bits cut from the candle card below are reassembled and put onto double-sided tape to make a charming and colorful background for the Day of Creativity.

Soft handmade papers cut to resemble candles are embellished with a computer-printed greeting and two brads.

■■ Artist Profile

Catherine Green,
Laminating

A career in interior design sparked in Catherine Green a passion for paper and textiles. Now, mixing textiles with new fibers, dying papers, cutting print blocks, and splattering paint are just a colorful day's work for Catherine. "I couldn't have hoped for a more fulfilling career to date," she says.

Catherine particularly enjoys working with textured handmade felts and luxurious velvet, but some of her recent pieces also incorporate painting and stitching on paper and fabric. She is constantly exploring new ideas and techniques, like mixing colorful iridescent fibers with wire, beads, and laminating techniques. Her work evolves as she discovers new materials, as well as new ways to use the old.

Catherine develops and sells her handmade cards, wedding stationery, and stitched pieces through her website (www.catherinegreen. co.uk) and at galleries and consumer shows.

L

LACE PAPER

See Paper or Washi Paper.

LAMINATE

A process of covering paper or fabric with thin, translucent plastic. Many forms of lamination are considered unacceptable as conservation methods, due to the high heat and pressure used during application.

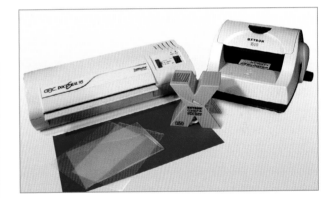

TYPES OF LAMINATE

Cold Laminate—An easy and inexpensive alternative to heat laminating. Convenient pre-sized sheets are now available to card makers through the Internet and from office supply and local craft stores.

Melamine laminate card

Cold laminate card

Melamine Laminate—Melamine is often used to fabricate countertops, providing a hard, durable surface. Laminate samples are often used in card making as miniature canvases, providing a hard surface for making charms or decorative embellishments. Melamine can be colored with alcohol or permanent ink, and used as a focal point or card accent.

Shell Laminate—This is a natural material used for decorative inlaid work. Adhesive-backed shell laminate provides artisans with a natural, beautiful color material, ideal for higher-end designed cards.

Shell laminate card

You can duplicate and figure out the many layers of masking by deconstructing this card image. Use multiple masks in several shapes, including cut-outs of the actual stamped image and scraps of square paper.

Torn scraps of computer paper appear as mountainous regions. Sponge with ink or chalk each layer to form the desert landscape.

MAT BOARD

A heavy fiberboard used to protect artwork or as a hard art-making surface. It is available in a wide variety of colors and textures.

Both of these cards were made using laser-printed acetate photos. When applied to metallic mat-board pieces, they provide an interesting multi-layered focal point.

MATRIX

A rigid, smooth, resin board placed in the vulcanizer with a metal plate and a sheet of rubber. When heated, the matrix material softens, and the images on the metal plate are pressed into the surface of the matrix board, which becomes rigid again when cooled. The result is a rubber stamp ready to cut, mount, and use.

MECHANICAL ELEMENT

A handmade, die-cut, or preassembled moving element that adds a decorative component, versatility, or function to a greeting card.

MEDALLION CARD

A single or multi-layered decoration placed on or near the center of a card as the focal point. Multi-layered elements may each differ in color or in paper stock. Each layer is often outlined or glittered to highlight it. *See also* Card Making.

More subtle than the blue daisy card, this stylized flower card was made much the same way. The most obvious difference is the dramatic analogous color scheme in darker values.

For this medallion card, begin by stamping, cutting, and coloring in the large image using watercolors, ink, or colored pencils. Cut the image out, leaving the bordering black lines, and mount it onto a stamped or printed paper surface. Notice the complementary color scheme and how it provides a pretty punch of color.

The Encyclopedia of Greeting Card Tools & Techniques

M

Melamine Laminate

See Laminate.

Melt Art

Three-dimensional accents created using a melting device and embossing powder, glue, or wax. Melted materials are poured into molds. *See also* Emboss.

Clip a Mica Tile to a Handi Clip and sprinkle silver embossing powder onto the surface. The clip will prevent your fingers from being burned as the tile is heated from the underside. Heating it from underneath prevents the powder from blowing away. While still hot, press an inked stamp, such as this snowflake, into the molten powder. When cooled, enhance the image by rubbing it lightly with mica pigments.

Memento

An item of remembrance passed on through a family. Parts of paper mementos are called ephemera, and are perfect visuals for card-making focal points.

Suze Weinberg,
Melt Art

An internationally celebrated rubber-stamp artist, Suze Weinberg began designing and creating with rubber stamps more than 18 years ago. While Suze may have started stamping as a hobby, she has since spent many years developing unique products for the rubber-stamp industry, including Ultra Thick Embossing Enamel, Wonder Tape, The Melting Pot, BeaDazzles, Mold 'n Pour, and dozens of others.

Suze is recognized not only as one of the founders of the American rubber stamp movement, but also for her expertise in develping the techniques of melt art. Both skills translate into wonderful greeting cards. Known for her years of product education, development, and editorial contributions, she also delivers an always informative and fun "Schmooze With Suze" newsletter and website (www.schmoozewithsuze.com).

Suze continues to write books, produce videos, and travel the world teaching techniques using the products that bear her name, all the while exploring new adventures, such as photography and computer technology. Taking a class or workshop with Suze is both a comedic and creatively joyful experience, as she teaches using humor mingled with expertise.

MEMORABILIA

A collection of remembrances, such as bits of paper ephemera or personal items that remind you of a special time, place, thing, or event.

Memorabilia card

MESH

A material characterized by its open, net-like appearance. Mesh may be made of fabric, jute, paper, or plastic. It's a popular textural element in card making.

METAL ART

A decoration made from various metals, including tin, pewter, or copper or other metal-like substances using aging patinas, and techniques such as embossing, debossing, repoussé, and etching.

Using a vinyl copper-colored sticker and metal mesh, begin by heating the mesh with a heat gun to alter the color. Apply the sticker and cut the entire image out. Use the mounting squares to raise the image, adhering it to a stamped and painted background.

A tin elephant coated with silver embossing powder is layered onto a marbled polymer sun and stamped background. Cut-outs of grass and Mica Flakes add even more texture and just the right finishing details.

The Encyclopedia of Greeting Card Tools & Techniques

heartfelt wishes

Ready-made molds or even rubber stamps can be used to provide a surface for creating textural metal borders, such as the one on "Mona Lisa Smile" or the focal point, such as on the "Heartfelt Wishes" card. To enhance the raised or debossed areas, use acrylic glazes, waxes, and hammered backgrounds using a small nail or tool. The background for "Copper Potter" was accomplished using an embossing stylus.

MICA

A transparent, flaky mineral with excellent heat-resistance, characterized by the formation of thin-layered sheets. Mica color ranges from colorless to black. When used with paint or attached to other pigments, it produces a wide range of iridescent, pearlescent, or metallic products. Colored mica particles and flakes are used as embellishments. *See also* Interference Mica.

Stamp and emboss a Mica Tile, using a large image such as this tulip stamp. From the reverse side, apply clear drying PPA-Gloss. In sections, apply the glue and Mica D'Lights. Then turn the tile over, revealing the finished "stained glass window" effect. Adhere the tile to a card, using a bit of shiny fiber for even more sparkle.

Adhered with a clear acrylic adhesive, larger bits of mica when colored appear as textural, glimmering, miniature brushstrokes of paint.

NEEDLEWORK

Designs done with a needle—by sewing, embroidery, needle-point, tapestry, quilting, or appliqué. Traditionally, card making needlework encompasses cross-stitch and needlepoint designs, but these days card makers have many templates available for intricate stitching techniques.

Cross-stitched squares, each depicting a different day in the Twelve Days of Christmas, make beautiful cards, which can later be framed.

Needlework templates

NEW BABY CARD

A card sent to celebrate a birth. New parents are usually overwhelmed, but always appreciate a thoughtful card. Make it a handmade card and surprise them. Here are some samples to show you several different approaches.

Congratulations

Tiny paper-quilled footprints are nearly as perfect as the real thing!

B A B Y

THIRTEEN

NEW YEAR'S CARD

While you might not think of New Year's Eve and New Year's Day as normal card-giving holidays, think of all the possibilities—new beginnings, resolutions, reminders, and just plain fun. Here is one fun idea for a card; there are many more throughout the book.

OIL CRAYON

A pigment mixed with slow or non-drying oils and/or wax binders. Oil crayons are far less powdery than traditional pastels, and performance is more like a typical wax crayon. When complete, oil crayon artwork on a greeting card must be protected with a fixative. Also called wax or oil pastels.

Tear blue masking tape to form stripes. Drizzle a resist—such as Perfect Paper Adhesive (PPA) or Crystal Lacquer—onto the card and allow it to dry thoroughly. Dribble oil crayons in random patterns onto Studio Paper or wax paper and turn it onto the card. Lightly press the oil crayon with a warm, dry iron. You may get several cards from one sheet.

OIL PASTEL

See Pastel.

ORGANIZATION

Having an orderly process to storing greeting cards. Everyone receives a few greeting cards a year that have sentimental value or are too pretty to toss. *See also* Box, Card Album, Framing, Recycling, and Repurposing.

If you don't want to throw out your new greeting cards, save them with style.

ORGANIZING TIPS

- Store new or handmade greeting cards in an expandable file or box with dividers.
- Label each divider so you can sort the cards by occasion or month.
- Keep a monthly holiday and birthday tracking calendar on the front of each divider, and make cards in advance, storing them in each occasion or monthly section.
- Clip your favorite pen to the front so that sending cards is quick and easy.
- Store return address labels and postage stamps in the front-most pocket.
- Keep your address book, or an easy-reference address list, in the front of the file.
- Make a category notation in your address book by each address that says "Christmas," "Birthday," or another holiday category or code. This list keeps you organized, providing a to-do list for future years.
- Scan or copy handmade cards to reference for future designs. Mark who you sent them to so that you don't inadvertently send a similar card.
- Keep an easy "drop in" envelope in one section. Use it for addresses torn from envelopes you receive. Once or twice a year, update your address book and easy-reference list.

ORIGAMI

The art of folding paper into representational shapes with dimension. While traditionally considered a Japanese paper art form, origami originated in China around the first century A.D.

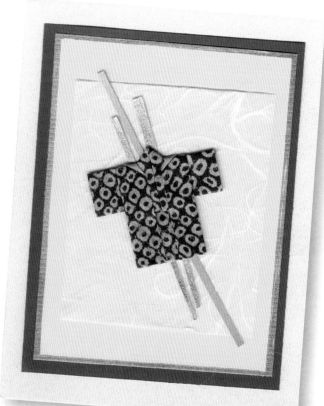

A BIRTHDAY BRINGS SUCH FUN AND CHEER TOO BAD WE HAVE BUT ONE EACH YEAR

Happy Birthday

HOW-TO BASICS: ORIGAMI HEARTS

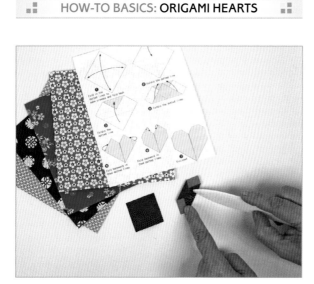

1. Begin this simple design, following the pattern and using your bone folder to make crisp folds.

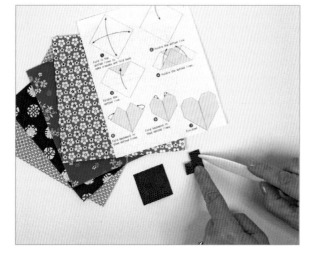

2. Finish each heart, using various colors of red and patterned papers to create more interest in design and texture.

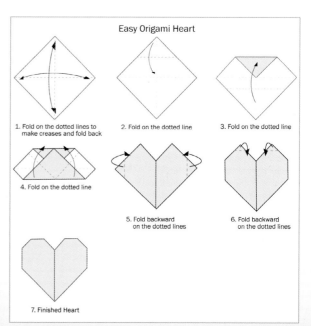

Notice the strong composition of this card, with its bold shapes and added geometry of fiber elements. The playful curvilinear line of the hearts gives this card its appeal.

Easy Origami Heart

1. Fold on the dotted lines to make creases and fold back

2. Fold on the dotted line

3. Fold on the dotted line

4. Fold on the dotted line

5. Fold backward on the dotted lines

6. Fold backward on the dotted lines

7. Finished Heart

Dozens of free origami patterns (like this one) are available online and in books. Follow some of the simpler patterns for cardmaking and assemble them as shown.

ORNARE

A technique in which a decorative template is placed on the reverse side of card stock, then pierced completely or partially through, using a pin or needle tool.

OVAL CUTTER

A specialized paper trimmer that cuts paper or photographs into oval shapes.

Ornare cards

P

PAINT

An art material made of pigment and binder. Pigment provides color to paint, and in its raw form it is ground. *See also* Acrylic Paint, Gouache Watercolor, Mica Watercolor, Specialty Paint, Watercolor.

Paint for greeting cards is made by many different manufacturers in an almost endless array of colors.

Acrylic painted card

PAPER

A material made of vegetable fibers composed of cellulose held together by hydrogen bonding. The most common source of paper fiber is wood pulp, but may also include cotton, hemp, linen, flax, and rice. *See also* Card Stock, Coated Paper Stock, Corrugated Paper, Embossed Paper, Paste Paper, Permanent Paper, Photo Paper, Printed Paper, Ready-Made Card Stock, Sticker Paper, Tissue, Vellum, Washi Paper, and Watercolor Paper.

Card stock

Metallic papers

The Encyclopedia of Greeting Card Tools & Techniques

PAPER ENAMELING

A technique in which the acrylic glossy product Perfect Paper Adhesive (PPA) is poured over artwork, such as paper collage, to form a thick opaque layer. When completely dry, the layer becomes crystal clear with a glass-like finish, resulting in artwork that resembles copper enameling. The technique was developed and the term coined by the author.

A paper-enameled card

PAPER FASTENER

Any utilitarian or decorative fastener made to hold cardmaking elements in place.

PAPER FOLDING

See Accordion Folding, Fold Out Card, and Moveable Card.

PAPER TRIMMER

A tool that works by aligning paper to a grid and sliding the small, razor-like blade on the built-in track, cutting the paper in a single movement.

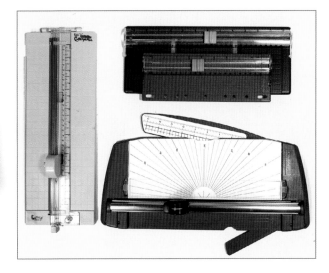

PAPER WEAVING

A technique of weaving paper strips in a method similar to weaving fibers. *See also* Weaving.

PAPUELA

The technique of inserting thin paper strips through slotted paper to create a woven-like pattern.

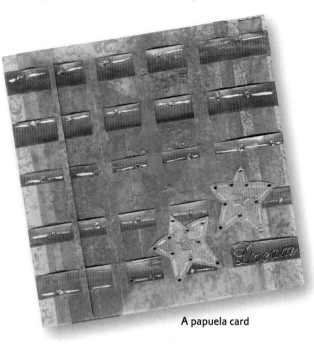

A papuela card

PARCHMENT CRAFT

Embossing, scoring, or piercing translucent paper, often vellum, to create delicate lace-like patterns. Also called pergamano.

PASTE

See Adhesive.

PASTE PAPER

A method of altering, texturing, and decorating a plain or patterned paper surface using one of several kinds of paint and common hand tools. *See also* Paper.

Paste paper is often prettier than a printed paper because it provides reflective texture. The process of making the paper is a pleasurable art form and one any card maker can enjoy, using acrylic paints, glazes, and traditional paste recipes.

TIP

Making paste paper can be a messy, but fun art form. Invite lots of friends and make a day of it. Have everyone make one style and then swap, increasing each person's stash of colored and textured papers for card making.

Paste Ingredients
Yield: 1 pint (2 cups) of paste
2 cups warm water
1 tablespoon methyl cellulose,
   rice starch, or cake flour

Creating the Paste
1. Pour 1 cup of the water into a medium-sized bowl and sprinkle in the methyl cellulose. Stir well. Set aside to thicken for about 1 to 2 hours, stirring occasionally.

2. Add up to ¾ cup more warm water, stirring until thoroughly blended. The mixture should be the consistency of unset pudding. If it is too thick, add up to ¼ cup more water.

3. Divide the mixture into several cups, depending on how many colors you want to use for your papers, and add approximately (you'll need to experiment) 1 tablespoon of color to each cup. Tempera, acrylic, gouache, inks, or dry pigments (matte or iridescent) all work well for color.

4. Store the unused portions in covered containers and refrigerate.

Application
1. Choose paper that is relatively smooth, not too absorbent, but able to withstand being wet—watercolor, recycled, or bond papers, for example.

2. For paler tones, dampen and relax the paper. For more intense colors, omit this step.

3. After you have applied the colors, use sponges, combs, carved plastic applicators, or brushes to make various designs in the paste. Set the papers aside to dry.

4. When the papers are completely dry, iron them from the back on several layers of newspaper. Do not use steam.

PASTEL

A squared or rounded stick of color, consisting of ground colored pigment and a binder. The pigments used in pastels are the same as those used to produce all paint. Pastels used in card making must be protected with a fixative.

Pastel crayons and pencils

TYPES OF PASTELS

- **Soft pastels** contain a higher percentage of binder to pigment, providing a greater ease of blending.

- **Hard pastels** contain a higher percentage of pigment to binder, providing a firmer and more defined drawing texture and detail.

- **Pastel pencils** are available in both a soft and hard pastel, encased in a wooden stick handle much like any pencil. These are ideal for artists with sensitivities to handling pigments or binders. Pastel pencils may be sharpened, and they produce less dust than traditional pastels.

- **Oil pastels** feature an oil binder and produce intense colors, though they are more difficult to blend.

With pastels, you can blend colors before you seal them with a fixative.

Pen

A handwriting or drawing implement containing an ink used in card making.

Pen and Ink

Drawing or writing in which ink is applied to paper using a pen or other stylus. It may be used as a medium for sketches, finished artwork, fine writing, and calligraphy.

Black and white line drawings lend themselves nicely to reproduction. This little seal was drawn and copied onto lightly textured card stock, then packaged as a small, boxed greeting card collection—a perfect gift for family and friends.

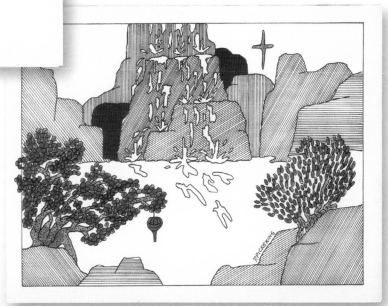

PENCIL

A drawing or writing tool made of natural powdered graphite and varying amounts of clay. Protect your pencil artwork with a fixative. *See also* Colored Pencil.

PERMANENCE

The ability of a material to resist chemical deterioration or changes in its properties. A proper storage environment plays a large part in a paper's permanence quality.

PERMANENT PAPER

The type of paper needed for absolute archival integrity, which means that it must last several hundred years. To be permanent, paper must: comply with Standard ANSI Z39.48-1984; have a pH level of 7.5 or greater; contain an alkaline buffer of calcium carbonate or another alkaline; be free of chemical impurities and, optimally, contain cotton or other rag fibers; be resistant to tears and folding. *See also* Paper.

PHOTO CARD

A greeting card that uses a single photographic theme, such as a person, pet, holiday, new home, spring garden, first car, or vacation.

Mica tile has natural color, providing additional vintage sepia color to old photographs and paper ephemera. Either put the elements under thin layers of mica, or sandwich them in between.

Photo cards

PHOTO CORNER

A self-adhesive paper triangle or decorative shape, used for mounting and easy removal of photographs or memorabilia.

PHOTO MOUNTING CORNER

A self-adhesive polypropylene, metal, plastic, or other material, often with a triangle-like shape, used for decoratively mounting a card element or photograph.

Photo mounting products have progressed way past basic black.

Mica is very versatile and can even be die-cut to form mounting corners and give a card composition a translucent organic design element. Naturally sepia-toned sparkling mica bits sprinkled onto embossing paste work well with mica corners.

A card with metal photo mounting corners

PHOTO PAPER

Paper made especially for inkjet or laser printing. Select photo paper for its brightness, weight, and finish. *See also* Paper.

PHOTO TAPE

A usually archival quality, permanent, self-adhesive tape with an easy-to-remove paper backing—also called a liner.

PHOTO TINTING

The technique of lightly applying color to a black-and-white or sepia-colored photograph, by using oil or other specialty water-soluble paints or markers. Besides the traditional photo-tinting techniques, much of the process can be accomplished today using the computer. Computer-generating photos and enhancing them mechanically can produce interesting and colorful results.

PIERCING

Pricking paper with a needle or needle-like tool for the purpose of creating a punched pattern. *See also* Ornare.

PIGMENT

A non-water soluble substance used to color ink, paint, paper, and textiles. Natural organic pigments are generally more stable than dyes, but produce a narrower color selection. *See also* Paint.

Examples of tinted photo cards

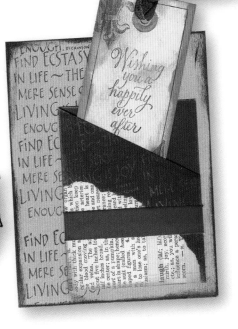

POCKET CARD

A card with a pocket added to or constructed into it.

Pocket cards can offer surprises of all kinds. This card holds a half-dozen mini-stick puppets. What child wouldn't like this in their Halloween sack?

Other pocket cards hold tags with the card's message.

POLISHED STONE

A paper coloring technique using permanent solvent-based ink, denatured alcohol, and gilding markers made by Krylon. When the ink is drizzled onto glossy or metallic card stock, dotted with the marker, and then blended with alcohol, the finished paper resembles polished marble. This technique and term, developed by artist Suze Weinberg, is often imitated using various other art materials, but seldom looks quite as spectacular.

TIP

Begin by having a play day! Spend time making piles of polished stone papers, keeping even those that seem less than successful. Use them to stamp on, making them into layered card borders or even into serendipity cards.

This card, covered with a stamped and inked piece of frosty vellum, showcases the brilliant polished stone technique and the interesting compositional juxtaposition of matte and glossy textures.

Simply stamped and embossed with gold powder, then mounted and corner-punched, this card was a favorite of all those who recieved it.

Spend some time experimenting with polished stone and resist techniques. The results are stunning and memorable cards.

POLYMER CLAY

A modeling material composed of resin, plasticizer, and occasional filler. Colorful, permanent, and water-resistant, polymer clay cures at a temperature of 265°F. It remains flexible when rolled thin and used for card making elements. *See also* Clay.

POLYVINYL ACETATE (PVA)

A vinyl polymer used in adhesive. Commonly called white glue or PVA, it is a safe adhesive as shown by its widespread use in schools. Bond time is immediate, although the tackier versions of PVA can take up to several hours to dry thoroughly. Dry time also depends on the thickness of application and the products being adhered. *See also* Adhesive.

Polymer clay cards

POP-UP CARD

A foldable greeting card, which in the folded position is relatively flat and fits into an ordinary mailing envelope. The front or inside of the card displays a decorative section that self-generates a three-dimensional, pop-up structure when the card is opened. *See also* Moveable Card.

While you can construct pop-up cards entirely by hand, manufacturers have produced products such as Popeze. This material is cut, made into a box shape, and applied to the card. A sticker, applied to a background paper, is the beginning of a pop-up.

POSTAL REGULATIONS

The rules for sending items by mail. Regulations vary by country, but some basic rules apply worldwide. Check the Internet for more specific information.

TIPS FOR ADDRESSING GREETING CARDS

- Use standard white, manila, or recycled paper envelopes.

- Send items needing extra protection in bubble-lined, padded paper, or waterproof envelopes.

- Include a return address on envelope.

- Write addresses parallel to the longest side of the envelope.

- Print or type addresses clearly with a pen or permanent marker.

- Do not use commas or periods.

- Use a post office box or street address, but not both.

- Include relevant directional references in addresses, such as "NW" for Northwest.

TO IDENTIFY SUSPICIOUS MAIL, LOOK FOR THESE SIGNS

- Powdery substance on the outside.

- No return address.

- An overuse of tape.

- Odors or stains on the envelope.

- A city or state in the postmark that does not match the return address.

POSTOID

A faux postage stamp created with art stamps and collage techniques. Do not use a postoid in place of regular postage.

PRESSURE-SENSITIVE ADHESIVE

An adhesive that bonds by both contact and pressure. *See also* Adhesive.

PRIMARY COLOR

See Color.

A BRIEF HISTORY OF QUILLING

While evidence of quilling dates back to Ancient Egypt or China circa 105 A.D., the first practical applications appeared in 15th century France and Italy when nuns and monks worked to form delicate paper filigree coils by wrapping them around bird feather quills. The quilled products decorated religious objects and were inspired by the leaf and flower petal motifs used in glass, ironwork, and woodcarving.

In the 18th century, quilling was taught to fashionable young Englishwomen alongside needlework. In America, quillwork decorated household items, pictures, trays, boxes, and other practical items. Quillers meticulously and artistically combined paper with shells, wire, fish nacre, and chipped mica. New England museums hold some of the remaining pieces, dating as far back as 1700.

For reasons unclear, quilling's popularity faded during the late 1800s. It made a limited resurgence in the 1950s, when it was shown decorating paper greeting cards or adorning framed documents. Women's magazines even featured paper filigree patterns in each issue.

QUILT

To piece together two or more pieces of fabric or paper. The technique involves four steps: piecing or cutting the pieces, layering or assembling the pieces onto a sub-surface, quilting (or, in card making, embellishing the paper pieces with pens, markers, thread, or other elements to simulate stitching), and binding, which involves gluing or taping the pieces together in card making. A quilt card can be made using simple geometric or more complex designs, following the traditional and contemporary style of quilting.

Once cut and assembled, this combination using an old watercolor and a sponged ink technique paper makes a contemporary quiltwork card.

QUOTE

A unique saying, scripture, verse, poem, or memorable word used to express a personal idea or sentiment. A quote can also acknowledge the card recipient's particular occasion. (For a selection of quotes and sentiments, see page 279.)

Printed machine-made paper scraps lend themselves to quilting. Piece together even the smallest and narrowest paper scraps to resemble traditional quiltwork.

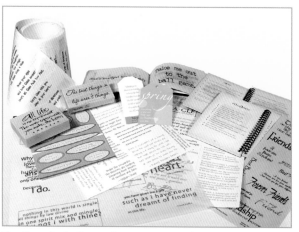

If calligraphy isn't your forte, you can still add nicely designed sentiments to your cards using these products.

A narrow piece of fabric quilting is repurposed from the much larger design and fits nicely into a window card. The olive-toned card stock and white card surface provide a balance of color. A fine-tip marker adds a repetitive border design as seen in the fabric. Rub-on type creates the sentiment.

Raffia

A natural fiber used in card making as an alternative to ribbon, providing a more casual or country appearance.

Ragged Edge

Unjustified copy. Usually, this refers to the right side of a paragraph of text.

Rag Paper or Board

A paper or board manufactured with a high content of long, cotton fibers, often used in high-quality card making.

Rainbow Pad

A rubber-stamp ink pad with several colors side by side, designed for multi-color stamping and brayer painting.

Random Act of Kindness

Sending a card or gift to someone anonymously, for no reason.

READY-MADE CARD STOCK

Blank cards and matching envelopes that can be transformed into a card for any occasion. Many ready-made varieties come embossed with borders, foiled with gold edges, or printed with geometrics. *See also* Card Stock and Paper.

Ready-made card stock and envelopes

RECYCLING

The act of reprocessing used or abandoned materials to create something entirely new. For card makers, this includes old greeting cards, paper, ephemera, and other objects.

TIPS

- Scan greeting cards onto your computer and recycle the real card.
- Carefully cut the main image into the shape needed for a craft, or into a tag shape for next year's gifts. Even the sentiment makes a nice gift tag. Throw away the rest of the card.

RED-EYE PEN

A pen specially made to take red-eye out of flash photographs.

REGISTER

The process of positioning two or more images so they are precisely superimposed. *See also* Stamp Positioner.

REINKER

A small bottle of ink made to refill stamp pads. May also be used independently for card making techniques that require wet colorants. Reinkers come in an array of colors and types, such as permanent, water based, hybrid, and solvent ink. *See also* Stamping.

Bits of Christmas wrap saved from year to year can be recycled for all kinds of paper craft projects. Here tiny bits were torn and attached to create a contemporary design. With a sprinkle of glitter or mica flakes, the tree literally glimmers, catching every light beam.

RELIEF EMBOSSING

See Dimensional Embossing.

REPOSITIONABLE ADHESIVE

A pressure-sensitive adhesive with a low tack characteristic, leaving minimal residue, staining, or damage when removed. *See also* Adhesive.

REPURPOSED CARD

A card made by using material that was previously used for another purpose.

Repurposed cards

REPURPOSING TIPS

- Cut off the front of a card and simply reattach it to a blank card so someone else can enjoy.

- Carefully cut the image and consider how it may look best: mounted onto colored stock, glittered, dimensionalized, or collaged into one to create a theme or quilt-like design.

Repurposing a seed packet into a greeting card gives cardmakers dozens of options. Use just the words, the flower photo, or, like the example, use the whole pack. Give it for any spring holiday or birthday. Or how about forget-me-nots for Mother's Day?

RESIST

A technique that preserves the white area of card stock. There are many techniques to cause paint or paper to resist color, from using wax-based colored pencils to traditional batik methods using paraffin wax and crayons. In addition, there are several liquid masking materials to paint or stamp with, such as Masquepen and Liquid Frisket, embossing powder resists, white glue or PPA (Perfect Paper Adhesive), and watercolor resists. This technique requires experimentation and patience, because often the design does not appear until after you've applied the wash and it has thoroughly dried.

1. Generously and evenly apply PPA to a piece of Cut 'n Dry. Using it as a stamp pad, stamp an image onto the paper. A shimmering gold card stock was used for this example.

Mix gum arabic and water to form a liquid paste. Stamp it onto glossy card stock and let it dry thoroughly. Sponge on alcohol-based inks. When dry, gently wipe the surface with a damp sponge, removing the gum Arabic. The white of the paper below shines through.

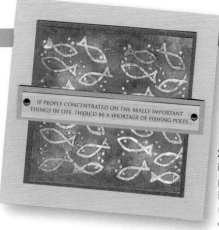

Stamp and emboss with clear ink and embossing powder. Apply inks over the surface, and, if necessary, buff the paper to remove excess ink. The white of the paper shows through the fish, which have resisted the ink.

The bold geometry of this Hot Potatoes stamp really shows off the full potential of the technique.

Apply a Masque Pen, PPA, or Crystal Lacquer to a stamp and press it to the paper. When dry, sponge on watercolors. When dry, buff or remove the masque resist by rubbing it off with your fingers.

2. When the PPA has dried, apply sparkling watercolors over the surface, allowing the colors to intermingle.

3. When completely dry, gently buff the paper with a cotton ball or tissue, revealing understated but beautiful stamped imagery, the gold paper shimmering through.

Another take on the technique also uses shimmering gold paper. This time, the stamp and emboss use clear embossing powder. Sponge a mica-based watercolor paint over the surface. Buff the art when dry, using a soft tissue, revealing perfect butterflies.

Draw a pattern onto watercolor paper using a fine point or paintbrush with PPA or Crystal Lacquer. When dry, apply traditional watercolors and dry. Add in more color using watercolor markers, and spritz the card to encourage the colors to bleed.

Apply stickers to paper and carefully rub stamping inks over the paper. Remove the sticker and apply others, creating multiple layers of design.

RHINESTONE

Though they are artificial gems, rhinestones often have facets that sparkle like a diamond. Originally, rhinestones were rock crystals gathered from the Rhine River in Europe. Today, crystal rhinestones are produced primarily in Austria by Swarovski. Inexpensive glass and plastic rhinestones are used as embellishment in card making.

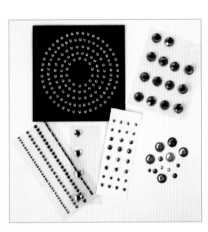

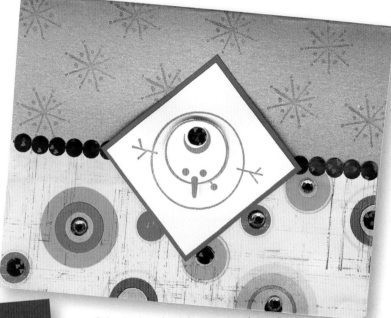

Selecting just the right papers and popping on some sticky-backed rhinestones and dazzle dots makes card making quick, easy, and sparkling!

RIBBON

A narrow strip of fabric, either finished at the edges or left ragged, used for embellishing, trimming, tying, or finishing a card composition.

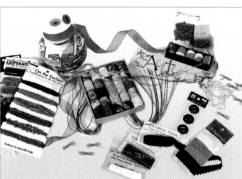

Ready-made adhesive-backed ribbon makes it easy to border window-cards, emphasize a card's greeting, or deck the halls and the tree.

Blue Ice by Kevin Nakagawa

Materials and Tools
Stamps (from Stampscapes)
Glossy card stock
Sponge applicators
White gel pen
Spray bottle
Dye-based inks in light blue, medium blue, dark blue, and black
Pigment ink in white

Instructions

1. Apply the ink from light blue to dark blue, layering each. The lightest colors should cover the entire card, but apply the darker colors on the left and right toward the outside edges only.

2. Apply the ink using a sponge and defined directional strokes, creating a streaky look.

3. When completely inked, lightly spritz the card with water. Where the water lands, the ink will lift, causing a bleached appearance and creating an illusion of deep space.

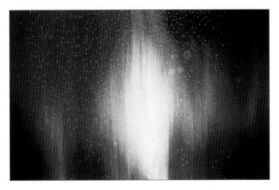

4. Stamp the foliage in three colors—light blue to create background branches, which will visually recede into the background; medium blue for the middle ground; and dark blue for the foreground.

5. Stamp additional branches using the black dye-based ink.

6. Stamp additional branches using the white pigment ink.

7. For additional details, use the white gel pen for the sky and the tips of the branches. These little dot details create a sparkle and introduce light back into the dark areas.

SCHERENSCHNITTE

(Pronounced *shair-en-shnit-teh*.) A scissor-cutting technique used to decorate birth and marriage certificates and create Christmas decorations. It became a popular folk art form in the 1800s.

Purchased in the Amish country and nearly 45 years old, this Scherenschnitte piece remained in the drawer until just the right moment. Finally mounted onto red card stock, it has been transformed into a charming wedding card.

SCISSORS

A hand tool used to cut paper, card stock, fabric, or other materials. Don't try to make greeting cards without one (or two).

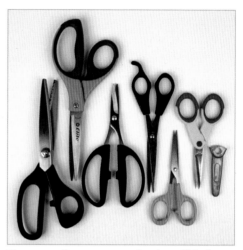

These are scissors every card maker will find useful. From left, they are pinking shears for cutting a fancy edge; shears for cutting card stock and mat board; Kai scissors for fatigue-free cutting; general scissors; children's scissors; and detail scissors with a safety cap.

SCORE

To crease paper with a burnisher or stylus, making it easier to crisply fold paper. Scoring allows card makers to make finished cards using scrap paper and discarded card stock.

HOW-TO BASICS: SCORING

Score your paper before folding it, and you'll get clean, professional-looking cards.

SCRAPBOOK

A blank book in which miscellaneous items such as greeting cards are collected and preserved. *See also* Organization.

SCRATCH ART

A technique of scratching into a surface, revealing the pattern or design underneath.

SCRATCH BOARD

A drawing board coated with white clay and a surface layer of black ink that when scratched or scraped away produces an effect similar to engraving.

Mica Tiles lend themselves to the scratch art technique because of their transparency and ability to receive color.

Glaze mixed with paint and applied to coated glossy stock slows the drying time. Slower drying means there's plenty of time to scratch in even the most intricate design. Use a paintbrush handle or orange stick for this style of card making.

S

SEALING WAX AND SEAL

A technique of impressing a design into hot wax using a metal die. The resulting disk features a pattern such as an image or letter.

SECONDARY COLOR

See Color.

SELF-HEALING CUTTING MAT

A composite mat designed to allow the use of rotary and straight utility blades without showing marks or cutting lines. Often the mat is printed with pre-calculated grid patterns and angles, making it ideal for designing and cutting card making elements.

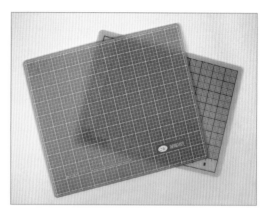

SELF-INKING STAMP

A stamp with an inkpad built into the handle. Commonly found in an office supply store, the tool may also provide uniquely fun words and titles for card makers. *See also* Stamping.

SEPIA COLOR

A dark brown ink or pigment traditionally prepared from the secretion of the cuttlefish, but now replicated using more common materials such as walnut ink, reinkers, paint, and glaze.

SEPIA PRINT

A photograph with a distinctive brown-to-olive-brown tint.

SEQUIN

A small, shiny ornamental disk, usually made of plastic, used for card making ornamentation and embellishing.

SERENDIPITY

A cardmaking technique in which handmade, collaged, stamped, inked, or pre-printed patterned papers are cut into geometric shapes, such as strips, squares, rectangles, and then randomly reassembled into different patterns and directions.

Serendipity cards

SEWING

As it pertains to card making, sewing is simply any hand- or machine-stitched paper or material added to a card. Similar to traditional sewing techniques.

After you've adhered all the small geometric shapes to the card stock, run the piece of paper through the sewing machine. It really has the look and feel of a quilt.

Ready-made papers, like those used behind the bunny sticker, come stitched with pretty threads and many patterns. These are easy to use for card making and will provide you with lots of ideas for sewing your own paper patterns.

SHABBY CHIC

A style of paper or embellishment that has a "worn from loving use" appearance. The term was coined by the interior design industry. *See also* Aging and Distressing.

HOW-TO BASICS: **SHABBY CHIC**

Use fine-grit sandpaper, an emery board, or a super-fine steel wool pad to distress edges or an entire piece of card stock and patterned paper, photos, plastic, or metal embellishments.

S

SHADOW STAMPING

A technique using color on a large, flat rubberstamp image that becomes the background composition for a focal point. *See also* Stamping.

HOW-TO BASICS: SHADOW STAMPING

Stamp with ink or paint and then add embellishments.

SHAKER CARD

A card making construction technique similar to a shakable snow globe. A shaker card usually is made with two or three layers: a decorative background; an acetate covered box; a cellophane envelope or other clear container containing "shakable" embellishments such as glitter, charms, and beads; and possibly a decorative top layer.

A shaker card

Examples of shadow stamping

SHAVING CREAM OR STARCH PAPER MARBLING

A technique for faux marbling paper using a liquid colorant and shaving cream or liquid starch.

1. Fill a shallow pan with about 1 inch of shaving cream. Level the cream with a ruler or paint stick.

2. Randomly drop two or three colors of liquid acrylic paint, stamp pad ink, or food coloring onto the shaving cream. Use a toothpick, the back end of a paint brush, or a texture tool to gently distribute the color into a swirl or marble pattern.

3. Gently push a piece of card stock onto the surface.

4. Carefully remove the card stock by holding one side or a corner. Continue to make more sheets using the same pan, skimming off and disposing the muddy colors. Marbled papers are beautiful when cut and used as a background for a focal point.

TIPS

Either use the paint stick to scrape off the remaining shaving cream, or allow it to turn powdery before buffing it off the paper with a paper towel. When scraping, use sweeping motions to avoid streaks in your design.

Even "muddy-colored" foam can be interesting, spread like icing onto card stock and allowed to air dry.

Shrink Plastic

A plastic sheet that—when it's heated—shrinks to approximately one-third of its original size and becomes approximately nine times thicker. Color applied to the plastic intensifies as the material shrinks.

1. Prepare your materials, including a heat tool, markers, ink, and the shrink plastic. Stamp the plastic, using permanent ink, and cut to size. Color in the design using a permanent marker. Press down the plastic with a metal heat tool holder, as shown, or other flat weight.

A card with a shrink plastic focal image. Because these pieces are so colorful when they shrink, they are often made into charms for jewelry. To do so, it is only necessary to punch a hole prior to shrinking, rather than afterward.

2. Begin heating the plastic. Hold it with a wood tool.

3. The plastic will shrivel and wad up like paper, but just keep heating. As soon as it relaxes, flatten the plastic with a heavy object.

SILHOUETTE

A drawing of the outline of a person or object, filled in with a uniform ink or paint color, usually black. Also, the use of a metal stencil to outline a design on dark paper that when cut and mounted resembles a silhouette.

HOW-TO BASICS: **SILHOUETTE**

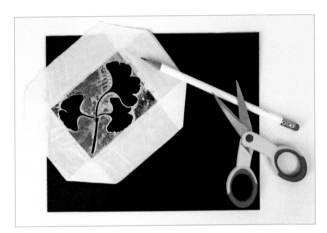

1. The materials are simple. Black paper, a pencil, a stencil, and sharp scissors are all you need. Just trace and cut.

2. After cutting the silhouette, use brads to mount it onto a piece of webbing-spray paper and ready-made card stock. A simple black rub-on finishes the card.

SLIDE MOUNT

Cardboard, plastic, and multicolored paper frames used as a compositional card element.

Slide mount cards

SLIDER CARD

A card construction technique in which an element is made to move or "slide" on a track or other mechanism, causing another element to be revealed, pop up, or cause movement.

SNAIL MAIL

Mail that is delivered by the traditional postal service, so-called because of the time it takes compared to sending something via e-mail.

SOFT PASTEL

See Pastel.

SOUVENIR

A keepsake that serves as a reminder. Meaning literally the "act of remembering" in French.

This fun, yet romantic card is a lovely reminder of a special dinner at a special restaurant. The heart medallion was a drink stirrer from an anniversary toast. On a card, it becomes a focal point and the sentiment itself—a nice souvenir and a nice memory. The background was created by smudging soft pastels over the background and drawing on a few pink hearts. It was sprayed with fixative before completing the card.

STAMP CLEANER

A tool with an applicator on top used to clean ink from stamps. To clean a stamp, use a gentle motion to apply cleaner, and then pat dry on paper towels.

STAMP POSITIONER

A two-piece device used for exactly lining up one rubber-stamped image over another. One piece is an acrylic L-shape, and the other a flat square of acrylic or acetate. Uses include: lining up elements such as borders and letters; precise alignment of a stamped image over a previously stamped image; and correcting an incomplete stamped image. *See also* Spritzing.

HOW-TO BASICS:
USING A STAMP POSITIONER

1. Place the L-shaped piece on the table.

2. Seat the acrylic sheet firmly against the two sides of the L.

3. Ink a stamp with pigment ink and fit it firmly against the two sides; then stamp.

4. Move the L away and align the image over the card stock. Place it exactly where you'd like to place the image.

5. Move the L back into place and hold it firmly in place.

6. Move the stamped acrylic away. Fit and stamp the inked stamp into the L's corner, perfectly aligning the image.

TIP

Stamping on thin acetate with permanent ink—saving rather than cleaning off the image—will eventually provide you with a bank of pre-stamped images that are always ready to go.

STAMPING

To reproduce the same image multiple times with a hand tool made of rubber, clear polymer, or other material, or a carved eraser or potato. *See also* Bleach, Clear Art Stamp, Foam Stamp, Hand-Carved Stamp, Mounted Stamp, Roller Stamp, Rubber Stamp, Self-Inking Stamp, and Unmounted Stamp.

STAMPING MAT

A durable foam work surface for stamping. A mat provides a slight "give," allowing for the best ink impressions, particularly for oversized stamps.

S

Dee Gruenig,
Stamping

You would think with eight books, nearly a dozen videos, hours of television work, thousands of classes, and at least 10 educational cruises, Dee Gruenig would slow down a little.

But those endeavors are just part of her creative life, which also includes designing and developing stamps and licensing stamping products with Sunday International, All Night Media, Marvy, Mrs. Grossman's Paper Company, Paper Adventures, Ott-Lite, Ranger, and her very own Posh Impressions, which she runs with her wonderfully organized and enthusiastic husband Warren.

What's next for Dee? "Sunday International and I have thrown ourselves into a single mission—to restore the excitement to rubber stamping," she says. "We really are beginning to 'grow up' a whole new generation of rubber stampers."

So Dee is doing even more—adding classes, workshops, and presentations to her already full roster of events, all the while demonstrating her remarkable designs using an EZ mount system.

4. After you've made an initial print and left it to dry, add more color to the rubber, spritzing and layering more color over the initial image. Using markers gives you the most options for precise color placement.

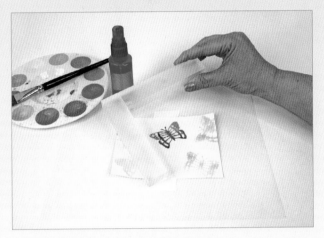

5. Start with lighter color choices and gradually build to a point of interest using stronger and darker colors. Building darker, more precisely placed color visually brings it to the front and pushes the others to the back, creating a sense of depth.

STATIONERS' HALL

The hall of the old Company of London Stationers, incorporated in 1557, which—until the Copyright Act of 1842—enjoyed the sole right of registering every pamphlet, book, greeting card, and ballad published. Although no longer compulsory, the practice of entering books at Stationers' Hall is still useful for reviewing copyrights.

STENCIL

A sheet of metal, plastic, cardboard, waxed paper, silk, or other material that has been perforated with a pattern. Ink or paint can pass through the perforations to create a printed pattern on the surface below. *See also* Bleach Stenciling.

HOW-TO BASICS: **STENCILING**

1. Align the stencil on the paper. It may be necessary to tape it in place.

2. Load a stencil brush with ink. When using paint, tap the brush onto a paper towel first.

3. Brush over the stencil openings with a light touch.

4. Carefully lift and move the stencil to the next section.

5. Wash the stencil and brush when complete.

After stenciling the design, use a craft knife and partially cut the pattern, lifting it to create dimension. Here a small lizard sports beautiful wire and bead jewelry.

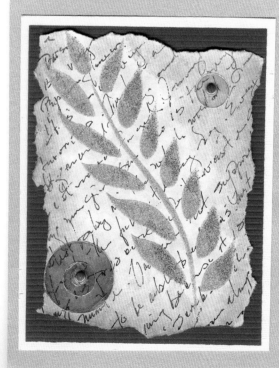

Use an old credit card or spatula to spread artist cement through the stencil. This technique produces a raised surface, perfect for sprinkling with glitter or mica bits. The background paper was stamped and then glazed in yellow ochre.

For a simple stencil, cut a heart shape into paper, and use a tiny stamp pad or sponge daubers to color it in.

STICKER

A decorative element with a gummed or adhesive backing. Double-sided stickers provide artisans with the opportunity to decorate the front or top of the sticker.

Double-sided stickers give you an opportunity to play with gilding, mica bits, glitter, microbeads, and flocking.

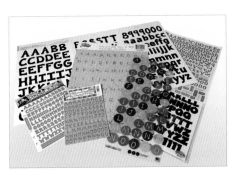

Single-sided stickers made by a sticker machine

STICKER MACHINE

A device that allows artists to make their own permanent adhesive-backed stickers.

STICKER PAPER

A label stock paper, suitable for printers, laser, stamping, watercolor, and rubber stamping. *See also* Paper and Sticker.

NOTE

No one uses sticker paper like artist Dee Gruenig (page 230). Dee stamps several sheets of the same design at a time, coloring and filing them according to stamp or subject.

TIP

When preparing sticker paper, keep several card elements handy and ready to assemble. Cut them out while you're on the phone or watching TV.

STIPPLING

A method of applying tiny dots of color with the tip of a brush to create a textured effect that simulates a fine, sandy appearance. Also known as pouncing, this technique is also suitable for adding subtle color and glazing.

STREAK

Stamping an image, then dragging the stamp without lifting, in order to create the feeling of movement.

STUDIO PAPER

A special paper that can be printed with an image using a computer and inkjet printer. The image can be transferred onto card stock by rubbing with a tissue or cotton ball. *See also* Transfer.

HOW-TO BASICS:
STUDIO PAPER TRANSFERS

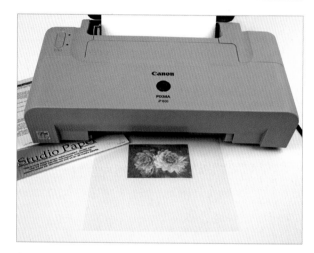

1. Insert the paper into your inkjet printer and print your favorite photo or portrait onto the paper.

TIP

For best results, set the printer on "best" or "photo" so it lays down the maximum amount of ink. If you are printing words, make sure to set the printer on "mirror image."

2. Turn the paper onto card stock and burnish the photo area with a burnishing tool or bone folder. Lift carefully at a corner to check if the transfer is complete. Take your time with this.

3. Lift and wipe the remaining ink off the Studio Paper. You can reuse it many times and on both sides.

4. Trim and use your transfer immediately or manipulate the color using a wet paintbrush.

STYLUS

In ancient times, a stylus was a pointed writing tool used to inscribe wax or clay. The Sumerians used a wedge-shaped stylus for their cuneiform writing. In the medieval period, a stylus was a pointed writing tool used for ruling a manuscript. Today a stylus is a small hand tool with a blunt rounded end used to emboss or deboss paper.

SWAP

Making multiples of cards, bookmarks, postcards, etc. for the purpose of swapping with others in order to acquire many different cards. When planning a gathering for making swaps, a host or hostess will often select one or two themes that all cards in the swap must follow. It is considered correct to send the swap hostess a card or small gift.

SWIVEL BLADE

See Craft Knife.

An image on studio paper can be transferred onto card stock to make numerous cards.

friends forever

S

TAG ART CARD

A technique using a tag of any size, shape, or weight as a card or a surprise element inside a card.

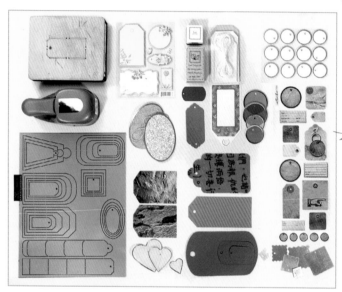

Jean Harley Shackleford,
Textiles

One part of Jean Harley Shackelford's creative inspiration goes all the way back to an important childhood lesson. "My mother always insisted on the importance of handwritten notes, whether it's a thank you, birthday or how-do-you-do," says Jean, who has a Master of Fine Arts degree from Savannah College of Art and Design.

It's a notion she carried through her education and into adulthood. It's the foundation on which she built a career, going from simply writing notes to making and marketing her own line of greeting cards: Bobbin Designs.

Named for her great-grandmother, Jean's line of cards features charming creatures bedecked in jewels and feathers, quilted, hand-stitched, and otherwise embellished. "Each piece is handcrafted, evoking an optimistic, happy-go-lucky sentiment," she says.

Kate's Paperie in New York City and Gump's in San Francisco carry Jean's cards, which she says are inspired by "random ideas that happen while falling asleep on the train or at some bizarre random moment."

Now, isn't that how everyone creates?

TEXTURE

To impart a desirable surface characteristic or distinctive pattern. In card making, you can create texture by using a variety of paper craft techniques, tools, and materials.

In these three examples, artist cement was used to create a textural, fluffy appearance. Begin by tracing a stencil or stamping an image. Fill it in using the artist cement, a craft stick, and toothpicks. Embellish the card with watercolor, buttons, and chalk once it is dry.

TEXTURE PLATE

A flat sheet of rubber, plastic, or other material used to create textural patterns on surfaces such as paper, clay, and metal.

Condition gold-colored polymer clay, then run it and a texture plate through a pasta machine. When baked, the flat image produces a lovely textural background that may be further manipulated with mica pigments and inks.

Textured card

THANKSGIVING CARD

A card you send to family and friends for the Thanksgiving holiday (celebrated on different days in the U.S. and Canada). You might not think to send a card for this day, but if you can't be there in person, a handmade card is the next best thing. Here are a couple of samples to show you just how. *See also* Holiday Celebration Card.

THANK YOU CARD

This is a card you send to thank someone for a generous gift, a thoughtful gesture, some needed help, or even another card! Thank you cards make up a significant portion of non-holiday cards. Here are some samples to get your mind working. *See also* Special Occasion Card.

thank you

Thank You

thanks

Thank You

THERMO ACETATE

A clear plastic that you can stamp, emboss, or use as a window for a shaker card. Thermo acetate can withstand the heat of embossing.

THERMOGRAPHY

A technique that uses a stamped image, ink, or gilding adhesive with thermal embossing powder to create a raised image when heat is applied. Also known as thermal embossing. *See also* Emboss, Embossing Powder, Heat Embossing.

HOW-TO BASICS: **THERMAL EMBOSSING**

Materials and Tools
Antistatic pad
Paper
Pigment ink, embossing ink, or gilding adhesive
Rubber stamp(s)
Embossing powder
Scrap paper for collecting the powder
Small dipper or spoon
Heat tool
Soft brush

Instructions
1. Lightly wipe the antistatic pad across the paper to absorb oils, moisture, and static.

2. Apply the ink or gilding adhesive onto an applicator (like a rubber stamp) and transfer that to the working paper surface. How you apply the ink or adhesive may vary depending on your creative objective. Stamps are the most common form of application, but you can also use a brush, brayer, or some other implement. If using a stamp, apply a uniform pressure.

3. Sprinkle a small amount of embossing powder over the stamped image.

4. Tilt the card, allowing the powder to spread across the image and adhere to the wet or tacky areas.

5. Dump the excess powder back into a container, and gently tap the back of the paper, removing tiny embossing particles.

6. Heat the powder until it melts, using a slow, steady sweep and targeting the embossed areas.

7. When cool, use a soft brush to remove any excess antistatic material.

8. You can leave the design as it is or color it with watercolor, pencils, paints, or chalks.

THERMAL EMBOSSING TIPS

- Avoid rocking the stamp, which creates shadow images.
- Work on a padded surface to obtain a good image using less pressure.
- Remember that different papers and inks have varying drying times.
- Drying speed is affected by humidity and the amount of embossing powder you use.
- Don't overheat the embossing powder, which can cause it to lose definition and shape.
- Don't overheat the paper, which can cause it to curl or burn.

A thicker embossing powder provides a raindrop effect, which is especially pretty on a marbled background.

THINKING OF YOU CARD

The only card sent for no other reason than to connect with a friend or loved one. There is no better way to show you care than a handmade card. It'll brighten your day while you make it and their day when they receive it. Here are some samples to get you thinking. *See also* Special Occasion Card.

have a great day

thread your day with happiness

Just a note

Simply the Best!

wheresoever you go
go with all your heart
CONFUCIUS

thinking of you

Wishing you Blue Skies
and Sunny Days

THREE-DIMENSIONAL EFFECT

To add dimension in card making by using small, adhesive-backed foam risers (also known as bumpers), or foam double-stick tape decorative elements, stickers, and embellishments. *See also* Tape.

Stamp and emboss an image such as these delicate palm fronds onto a heavyweight card stock. Use detail scissors to carefully cut around the fronds, and then lay them facedown in the palm of your hand. Roll a pencil over the fronds, giving them a delicate curl. Adhere foam risers to the curves, and mount the frond onto a watercolored card. Add mica flakes and bits to achieve a natural landscape.

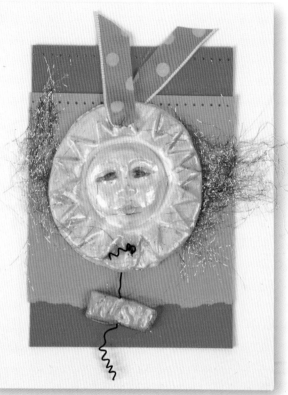

Air-dry clays offer card makers diversity when creating dimensional cards. Press the clay into a mold, or use a button, cookie cutter, or anything with texture to create a dimensional card focal point.

TISSUE

A soft, thin, usually translucent paper, available in many colors and patterns, used for collaging or as a card insert or overlay. *See also* Paper.

TIP

Select both bleeding or non-bleeding tissue papers, as each performs different tasks. Spritzing or wetting the bleeding type of tissue provides watercolor-like effects. Non-bleeding tissue tolerates a delicate, but wet adhesive.

TOOTH

A slight surface texture caused by the pressure of certain rollers during the paper's manufacturing process. A paper's tooth grabs and holds pastels and chalk.

TRADE CARD

An advertising card issued before 1900 by merchants who gave them away in products or with the purchase of a product. Trade cards were popular before the advent of the postcard, and often were collected and glued into large scrapbooks with other die cuts.

Cards using tissue paper

Trade cards

TRANSFER

To move an image from one place to another. Transfer techniques range from methods that require special chemicals and mediums, to easy processes using inexpensive, non-toxic, readily-available materials. *See also* Inkjet Transfer Paper, Rub-on Transfer, and Studio Paper.

With transfer paper and tools, everyone can create artistic cards.

Card with transferred images

CELLOPHANE TAPE TRANSFER

1. Apply a piece of wide shipping cellophane tape onto a photocopied image. Rub it down thoroughly with your thumb.

2. Soak the paper with water, and rub it off with your finger. The transfer will be on the cellophane.

3. Adhere it to the card as is, or trim around the image and use it as a laminate or collage element.

TRANSFORMATION

A card featuring a scene composed of vertical slats. By pulling a tab on the card's side, the slats slide under and over one another to transform into a totally different scene. *See also* Moveable Card.

TRANSLUCENT

A material that transmits light, but causes enough diffusion to prevent perception of distinct images; a state between transparent and opaque.

TRAPEZE STRING ART

The technique of suspending decorative elements, such as die cuts, embellished designs, and small collages, in and on decorative thread.

TRI-FOLD CARD

See Fold-Out Card.

TYPEFACE

The style of typed letters used for the body text of a greeting card.

Stamp and emboss onto vellum, taking care to hold the heat tool away from the paper to prevent it from curling.

TIPS FOR USING VELLUM

- Store vellum flat in a folder or box. Any crease or marring will damage the vellum and appear bright white.

- To emphasize a special card feature, layer vellum over the card, cutting away the vellum to reveal the special feature. The majority of the card becomes translucent, and the special feature is in sharp focus.

- Color vellum with chalks, either on the front or the back side.

- Use your computer to print the card message onto vellum.

- Use vellum to create special stickers, punches, or die cuts. Embellish them with glitter or mica bits.

- Adhesive and ink do not absorb as quickly on vellum as on regular paper. Before gluing vellum to paper, look for ways to use a non-permanent mount such as brads, stickers, ribbons, and punched areas.

- Use adhesive, tape, or glue stick very sparingly and apply them to the paper rather than the vellum.

- Use a permanent pen when writing or drawing on vellum.

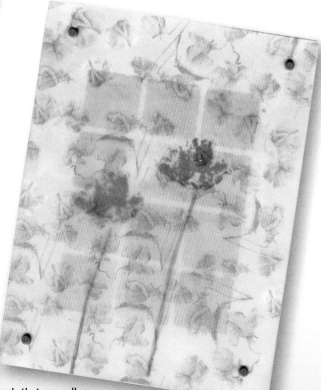

More cards that use vellum

Victorian

Of or pertaining to Queen Victoria I or the period of her reign from 1837 until her death in 1901. Also, the highly ornamented style of architecture, decor, art, and fashion popular in 19th-century England.

Vintage

Characterized by excellence, maturity, and enduring appeal; classic.

A card from circa 1945

May your life with blessings teem
And your cares be but a passing dream

A card from the early 1900s

May the fan of this girl
Cheer your heart and soul

Let it sway and twirl
And make you laugh and roll

© 1998 H. FISHLOVE & CO. PRINTED IN CHICAGO U. S. A.

This unusual Christmas greeting card has ooh-la-la appeal when you blow on the feather.

The

FAN DANCER

Season's
Greetings

You're the One ~~

A card from the early 1930s

W

WALNUT INK

Walnut ink crystals and water are mixed to a desired level of darkness, and when applied to the paper cause it to appear instantly aged. Dropping raw crystals directly onto dampened paper creates interesting dappled effects.

Walnut ink: another tool in the card maker's box

WARM COLOR

See Color.

WASH

A layer of color, often uniform in tone, applied across the paper with a brush or sponge. *See also* Color Wash.

WASHI PAPER

A type of paper traditionally made in Japan from the bark or fibers of the kozo or mitsumata shrubs and the gampi tree. Washi paper may also contain hemp, bamboo, straw, and other vegetative material. Also called mulberry or lace paper. *See also* Paper.

TIP

Delicate washi papers appear nearly opaque when layered and gently tacked over an image. An acrylic adhesive, such as PPA, firmly adheres the washi paper to the surface, nearly integrating it with the paper below and leaving the beautiful textural pattern, but very little white color.

WATERBRUSH

See Bleach Waterbrush.

WATERCOLOR

A paint in which water is used as the vehicle for carrying the pigment from the brush to the paper. Quality watercolors are made with pigments, not dyes, making them more lightfast. You can mix watercolor from tubes with those on a palette or in a pan and in conjunction with watercolor markers. You can mix watercolor with gouache to provide a base of color for pastels, pencils, and markers. Good watercolors contain emulsifiers that aid in rewetting and in providing smooth color transitions. *See also* Gouache Watercolor.

Gentle washes, leaving lots of white paper untouched, give an illusion of snow without using white paint. Boldly painted trees and the speedy skier emphasize the real scale of such a vision.

After stamping with permanent ink, spritz water directly onto the watercolor paper. Add touches of paint, manipulating it so that every edge bleeds into the others. To avoid muddying the paint, don't over-manipulate it. If you do, however, blot the paint with a paper towel and try again.

This watercolor technique provides the illusion of a school of fish, emphasizing the one swimming perilously close to the viewer.

Interference watercolors provide the most ethereal and beautiful color on dark card stock. The background paper was stamped simply. The central image was stamped, embossed in black, and painted. This card is suitable for any occasion.

WATERCOLOR

Sparkling watercolors produce amazingly luscious works on dark and light-colored card stocks. To use traditional watercolors on dark paper, mix in some sparkling mica-based paints.

Traditional watercolors produce instant and beautiful results. Notice how the artist edged the card in the same red as the holly berry, providing just the right framing.

Cy Thiewes,
Watercolor Artist

One of the better watercolor artists working in greeting cards today is Cy Thiewes. Having retired at 73, Cy moved to Sun City West, Arizona, where she found a wonderful place to develop her creative endeavors. She was thrilled when someone shared with her that nothing has to go to waste. "In fact," Cy says, "I found that not only was I given permission to tear out the good parts of my old paintings and recycle them into something else, but that it was perfectly acceptable!" For Cy, "Making cards was a result of not wanting to 'waste' my paintings. When you grow up being forever told that there is no such word as can't, it is often a nice surprise to see the result when you just jump in to try something new."

Cy's brilliant use of watercolors, ink, plastic wrap and acrylic paint "waste not" cards are beautiful enough to frame, but made to be given. She is one of those people who joyfully just "jumps in."

WATERCOLOR PAPER

A paper made of any natural fiber, usually cotton. Rag indicates the content of the paper; a rag content of less than 100 percent means that synthetic fibers or wood pulp are a part of the blend.

TIP

Cards are relatively easy to make, but what about matching envelopes? Strathmore is among the manufacturers now giving card makers the option to purchase heavyweight, textured, cold press watercolor cards, which are perfect for any wet media, including marker, acrylic, gouache, and watercolor. The matching envelopes even have a deckle edge.

WATERCOLOR PEN

A plastic-barreled brush that can dispense liquid through a brush tip. The barrel can be refilled with color, bleach, water, or other fluid material.

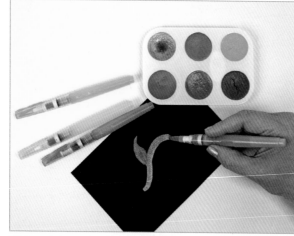

Watercolor pens in action—the color of the pen stock is purely decorative; you can fill a pen with any color.

WATERCOLOR PENCIL

A watercolor paint in a solid form, encased in a pencil. Watercolor pencils may be used independent of water, dipped in water, washed over a watery surface, or used with watercolors themselves.

Watercolor pencils come in as many colors as normal watercolor paints. They're easy to blend together, too.

Two watercolored cats cuddle together to view the magnificent skyline created with watercolor pencils. The textural contrast is a nice touch and makes a strong compositional statement.

WATERMARK

A patterned modification made during the formation of a sheet of paper while it is still wet. The pattern, design, or word can be seen in the dried sheet when held up to light.

WATERPROOF OR WATER RESISTANT

A material's ability to resist change when in direct contact with water. This includes, but is not limited to: softening, migration, swelling, bleeding, or dissolving.

WATER SOLUBLE

A material that dissolves in water.

WAX OR OIL PASTEL

See Oil Crayon.

WEAVING

To construct a card or card element by interlacing or inter-weaving strips or strands of fiber, ribbon, or paper.

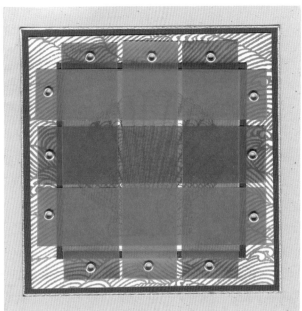

Weaving vellum offers an added bonus. The natural translucency of the material means the colors show through one another, causing a third or fourth color, depending on which one is on top or underneath the other.

Cutting and weaving pretty stamped papers give card artists a myriad of ways to use those scraps. This card is suitable for many occasions.

WEDDING CARD

A card given to a bride and groom on their special day. You can find the sentiments you want to share in a commercial card or you can simply make the card yourself. Maybe it'll touch the new couple so much that your card will end up in their wedding album. *See also Special Occasion Card.*

The Encyclopedia of Greeting Card Tools & Techniques

may your life
together
be full of *love*
and your love
be full of *life.*

A life of love and laughter; happily ever after.

WET ADHESIVE

Any adhesive that is applied while still in liquid form and dries to a solid to achieve its full bond strength with another material. *See also* Adhesive.

WINDOW CARD

Card stock with a die-cut aperture in nearly any shape, functioning as a window to fill or see through.

Crackled finished paper, stamped and rubbed with glaze, has an old-world appearance. When combined with subtle color and a triple-cut window, it produces a Grecian garden look.

April 1	Victory Day	Spain
April 1	April Fool's Day (All Fool's Day)	Great Britain, USA
April 7	World Health Day	UN member nations
April 22	Earth Day	USA
April 27	Freedom Day	South Africa
April 30	Queen's Birthday	The Netherlands
April 30	Walpurgis Night	Germany, Scandinavia
Last Friday in April	Arbor Day	USA, Belgium, The Netherlands, South Korea, Taiwan

May 1	May Day (Labor Day)	Most of Europe and Latin America
May 5	Cinco de Mayo	Mexico, USA
May 8	V-E Day	Europe
May 10	Mother's Day	Mexico
Second Sunday in May	Mother's Day	USA
Third Saturday in May	Armed Forces Day	USA
Last Monday in May	Memorial Day	USA
First Monday on or before May 24	Victoria Day	Canada

June 1	Children's Day	Worldwide
June 14	Flag Day	USA
June 16	Youth Day	South Africa
Third Sunday in June	Father's Day	USA (celebrated on different dates worldwide)

July 1	Canada Day	Canada
July 4	Independence Day (aka Fourth of July)	USA
July 14	Bastille Day	France

August 9	National Women's Day	South Africa

First Monday in September	Labor Day	USA
First Sunday after Labor Day	Grandparents Day	USA
September 16	Independence Day	Mexico, Papua New Guinea
September 24	Heritage Day	South Africa
late September–early October	Oktoberfest	A two-week festival held each year in Munich, Germany
September or October	Yom Kippur (aka Day of Atonement)	Jewish (celebrated on different dates each year)
163 days after Passover	Rosh Hashanah (aka Jewish New Year)	Jewish (celebrated on different dates each year)

October 24	United Nations Day	UN member nations
October 31	Halloween	Celebrated in most of the Western world

November 1	All Saints' Day	Observed by Catholics in most countries
November 1	Día de los Muertos (Day of the Dead)	Spanish (celebrated in many parts of the world)
November 2	All Souls' Day	Observed by Catholics in most countries
November 5	Guy Fawkes Day	UK
First Tuesday after first Monday of the month	Election Day	USA

November 11	Veterans Day	USA
Fourth Thursday in November	Thanksgiving Day	USA

December 16	Day of Reconciliation	South Africa
December 25	Christmas Day	Widely observed in all Christian countries
December 26	St. Stephen's Day	Austria, Ireland, Italy, San Marino
December 26	Boxing Day	Canada, Australia (except South Australia), UK, Northern Ireland
December 26–January 1	Kwanzaa	USA
December 31	New Year's Eve	Celebrated throughout the world

Chinese Holidays

Month 1, Day 1	Chinese Lunar New Year
Month 1, Day 15	Lantern Festival—End of New Year Festivities
April 4/April 5	Qing Ming Jie—Enjoyment of Spring Greenery
Month 5, Day 5	Dragon Boat—A historical boat racing day
Month 7, Day 7	Qi Xi—Chinese Valentine's Day or Magpie Festival
Month 7, Day 15	Ghost Festival—Festival of releasing miniature paper boats and lanterns on water representing a connection between the living and the dead
Month 8, Day 15	Mid-Autumn Festival—Celebration of abundance and togetherness, dating back 3,000 years
Month 9, Day 9	Double Ninth Festival—A day to drive away danger and a celebration to show respect for the elderly

Christmas Greetings
around the world

COUNTRY	GREETING
Brazil (Portuguese)	*Boas Festas*
Denmark	*Glaedelig Jul*
Finland	*Hauskaa Joulua*
France	*Joyeux Noël*
Germany	*Frohe Weihnachten*
Greece	*Kala Christouyenna*
Hawaii	*Mele Kalikimaka*
Ireland (Gaelic)	*Nolag Sona Duit*
Italy	*Natale allegro*
Japan	*Shinnenomedeto*
Navajo	*Merry Keshmish*
The Netherlands	*Vrolijk kerstfeest*
Philippines	*Maligayang Pasko*
Poland	*Wesolych Swiat*
Portugal	*Christmas Alegre*
Romania	*Sarbatori Fericite*
Russia	*Vesyoloye Rozhdyestvo*
South Africa (Afrikaans)	*Geseende Kerfees en 'n gelukkige nuwe jaar*
Spain	*Feliz Navidad*
Sweden	*God Jul*
Thailand	*Sawadee Pee Mai*
United States	Merry Christmas
UK	Happy Christmas

Quotations & Sentiments

VALENTINE'S DAY

Valentine's Day was made for people like you...
For wherever you go, you bring love.
Happy Valentine's Day

Know what, Valentine?
You're almost as sweet as chocolate!
Happy Valentine's Day

Your love has made my days brighter and more beautiful.
Happy Valentine's Day

Right from the start ... you stole my heart!
Happy Valentine's Day

Love!
Just one word, but it says so much.
Happy Valentine's Day

Know what I like about you?
Everything!
Happy Valentine's Day

CHINESE NEW YEAR

Wishing you Prosperity and Good Luck
in everything you do

May each day be filled with happy moments, warmth,
laughter, and togetherness, too.
Happy New Year to you

Wishing you a grand, glorious, and prosperous beginning
to another year—Happy New Year

May the first rays of the sun this New Year bring you
happiness and joy.

ST. PATRICK'S DAY

For each petal on the shamrock
This brings a wish your way—
Good health, good luck, and happiness
For today and every day.
—Author Unknown

May your blessings outnumber
The shamrocks that grow,
And may trouble avoid you
Wherever you go.
—Irish Blessing

Never iron a four-leaf clover.
You don't want to press your luck.
—Author Unknown

If you're enough lucky to be Irish,
you're lucky enough!
—Irish Saying

May your pockets be heavy and your heart be light,
may good luck pursue you each morning and night.
—Irish Blessing

PASSOVER

As you break matzo with those you love,
may you always find peace and hope in your hearts.
Happy Passover

EASTER

Easter is one time when it's safe
To put all your eggs in one basket.

Somebunny Loves You!

Just poppin' in
To wish you a hoppy Easter!
Happy Easter

You're wished a basketful of
Bright springtime smiles.
Happy Easter

Rejoice in the Lord!
May all the beauty and glory
Of this blessed season
Fill our hearts with praise.
Happy Easter!

Let us give thanks to the risen
Lord for His glorious gift of life.
Wishing you a Blessed Easter Season.

At this glad time may your heart enjoy a sweet
renewal.
Happy Easter

EARTH DAY

Celebrating with you!
Sharing the beauty and wonder of our planet.

Come together. Let's share a peaceful world.

Let's reach out to all we know
to make our World more Beautiful.

CINCO DE MAYO

Viva Cinco de Mayo!

The years may keep changing
But our Spirit remains the same.
Have a Grand Cinco de Mayo.

MOTHER'S DAY

A mother's duty:
Give your children roots,
Then give them wings.

A Mother holds her children's hands for a while …
And their hearts forever.

God invented mothers because
He couldn't be everywhere.

God made you my Mother …
Love made you my Friend.

House Rules:
#1. Mom's the Boss.
#2. See Rule #1.

Mothers are the roses in the garden of life.

FATHER'S DAY

Anyone can be a dad—
But it takes a man to be a father.

I'm just as lucky as I can be
For the world's best Dad belongs to me.

You're the "bestest" grandpa in the whole wide world!
Happy Father's Day

Thanks for giving me the finer things in life,
your time and your love.
Happy Father's Day

Dad, your life has made such
a wonderful difference in mine!
Happy Father's Day

INDEPENDENCE DAY

God bless America
... please hurry!
Home of the Brave

Hurray for the Red, White, & Blue!

Old Glory ... Long may she wave!

HALLOWEEN

Bbb...Bbb...Bbb...BATS all folks!

Broomrides ... 25 cents!

I do believe in ghosts.
I do, I do, I do!

I thought I'd like to be a witch,
So, I tried it for a spell ...

No Tricks ... Just Treats!

Trick or Treat ...
You're so sweet ...
Please give me something ...
Good to eat!

THANKSGIVING

Count your blessings.

Feast with the Pilgrims.

Gather together ... with thankful hearts.

Giving thanks for the simple things in life.

Gobble 'till you wobble!

Have a good fall
Y'all!

May the bounty of the season fill your
Heart and your home.

Save a Turkey! Send out for Pizza!

Thanksgiving is not just a time of the year ...
It's an attitude of the heart.

WINTER

Free Snow!
Shovel all you want!

Snowflakes are kisses from heaven ...

A Snowman's Prayer.
Please freeze.
Amen.

CHANUKKAH

Shalom
Peace to You
at Chanukkah
and Always

A Chanukkah Wish for You
May the traditions of old bring you new joy.

Chanukkah ... A tradition of freedom,
Courage and peace.
A time of renewed faith and hope.
Have a Joyous Celebration.

KWANZAA

No man is an island, entire of itself,
Every man is a piece of the continent.
—John Donne

Remember upon the conduct of each
depends the fate of all.
—Alexander the Great

Unity to be real must stand the severest strain
without breaking.
—Mahatma Gandhi

Sticks in a bundle are unbreakable.
—Kenyan Proverb

A snowflake is one of God's most fragile creations,
But look what they can do when they stick together!
—Author Unknown

No man is free who is not a master of himself.
—Epictetus

We all participate in weaving the social fabric;
We should therefore all participate in patching the
fabric when it develops holes.
—Anne C. Weisberg

Faith is like radar that sees through the fog.
—Corrie ten Boom

The time is always right to do what is right.
—Martin Luther King, Jr.

RAMADAN

Peace to you this Ramadan

Have a Blessed Ramadan

CHRISTMAS

Christmas Cheer ... Welcome Here

Jesus—the reason for the season.

The sparkle in my child's eye,
of wonder and delight ...
Shines brighter than any Christmas lights,
glowing in the night.

Happy Yule, Y'all!!

Dear Santa: I want it ALL!!

May peace be more than a season ...
May it be a way of life.

Christ was born on Christmas morn!
May our Savior's birth so long ago
Bring peace and joy to your family today.

It's that magic time of year,
when everything is gentler and more beautiful.
Peace on Earth!

ANGELS

A kind soul is inspired by angels.

Angels are often silent,
but they are listening to every thought that stirs our
souls.

Angels don't disappear,
even if you pretend they don't exist.

Angels ...
Don't leave home without 'em.

An angel in the house they say,
will guard your family night and day.

An Angel is someone you feel like you've known
forever, even though you've just met.

LOVE & WEDDING

Two lives.
Two hearts.
Joined in friendship,
Together in love.

May your marriage continue to bless you
with the friendship and love that brought you
together.

To Love, Honor, and Cherish.

May your life together
begin with a beautiful today.

Congratulations on Your Wedding!
Here's wishing you every happiness as you begin your
life together.

Love comforteth like sunshine after rain.
—William Shakespeare

There is no remedy for love, but to love more.
—Thoreau

Love bears all things, believes all things,
hopes all things, endures all things.
—1 Corinthians

ANNIVERSARY

All my love ...
To the one who shares all my life.
Happy Anniversary!

Joining with you in celebrating another year in love.
Happy Anniversary

Love brought you together as husband and wife,
and gave each of you a best friend for life.
Happy Anniversary

May the life you share be filled with love.
Best Wishes for a Wonderful Life Together!

BABY

Today love has a name ...
Congratulations on the birth
of your brand new miracle!

To Hug and to Hold
From This Day Forward.

Babies are such a nice way to start people.
—Don Herrold

A baby is God's opinion that the world should go on.
—Carl Sandburg

People who say they sleep like a baby
usually don't have one.
—Leo J. Burke

HAPPINESS

Most folks are about as happy as they make up their
minds to be.
—Abraham Lincoln

The secret of happiness is to make others believe they
are the cause of it.
—Al Batt

Happiness is having a large, loving, caring,
close-knit family ... in another city.
—George Burns

Additional Resources

CARD ASSOCIATIONS

UK Greeting Card Association (UK)

www.greetingcardassociation.org.uk

Australian Greeting Card Association (AU)

www.greetingcardassociation.com.au

The Greeting Card Association (US)

www.greetingcard.org

BOOKS ON MAKING CARDS

Each of the following publications from Lark Books and Sterling Publishing contains numerous projects to inspire your own card-making endeavors.

50 Nifty Beaded Cards
Chris Rankin
Paper, 128 pages
Lark Books
ISBN 978-1-60059-146-4

50 Nifty Collage Cards
Peggy Jo Ackley
Paper, 128 pages
Lark Books
ISBN 978-1-60059-121-1

50 Nifty Quilled Cards
Alli Bartkowski
Paper, 128 pages
Lark Books
ISBN 978-1-60059-233-1

Artful Cards
Katherine Duncan Aimone
Paper, 144 pages
Lark Books
ISBN 978-1-60059-140-2

Classic Cards
Marrian Piers
Paper, 160 pages
Sterling Publishing
ISBN 978-1-4027-4739-7

Greeting Cards Galore
Mickey Baskett & Marci Donley
Paper, 128 pages
Sterling Publishing
ISBN 978-1-4027-5376-3

Handmade Greeting Cards for Special Occasions
Amanda Hancocks
Hardcover, 128 pages
Sterling Publishing
ISBN 978-1-4027-4026-8

Teeny Tiny Cards
Jane LaFerla
Hardcover, 128 pages
Lark Books
ISBN 978-1-60059-066-5

Vintage Pop-Up Cards
Taylor Hagerty
Hardcover, 128 pages
Lark Books
ISBN 978-1-60059-031-3

Manufacturers' Materials Reference

7 Gypsies www.sevengypsies.com

Alexx Kesh & Co. www.alexxkesh.com

American Greetings www.americangreetings.com

Art Gone Wild www.agwstamps.com

Art Institute Glitter www.artglitter.com

Artchixstudio.com www.artchixstudio.com

Bazzill www.bazzillbasics.com

Bella Press www.denamidesign.com

Clearsnap www.clearsnap.com

Club Scrap www.clubscrap.com

Comotion www.uptowndesign.com

Craf-t Products www.craf-tproducts.com

Crate Paper www.cratepaper.com

Creating Keepsakes www.creatingkeepsakes.com

DaisyD's www.daisydspaper.com

Delta www.deltacrafts.com

DeNami www.denamidesign.com

Designs By Dreamer www.designsbydreamer.com

EK Success www.eksuccess.com

Fiskars www.fiskars.com

Fragile Crackle www.synta.com/anita1.html

Fred B. Mullet www.fredbmullett.com

Golden Artist Colors www.goldenpaints.com

Hallmark Cards www.hallmark.com

Heidi Swapp www.heidiswapp.com

Heritage Handcrafts www.heritagehandcrafts.com

Home Studio International

   www.homestudiointernational.com

Hot Potatoes www.hotpotatoes.com

House-Mouse Designs www.house-mouse.com

Impression Obsession www.impression-obsession.com

Inkadinkado www.inkadinkado.com

Inque Boutique www.goinque.com

Innovative Stamp Creations

   www.innovativestampcreations.com

It Takes Two www.ittakestwo.com

Jacquard www.jacquardproducts.com

Jolees www.eksuccess.com

Judikins www.judikins.com

K & Company www.kandcompany.com

Ken Brown of Rubber Stamps of America

   www.stampusa.com

Kopp Designs www.koppdesign.com

Krylon www.krylon.com

Magenta www.magentastyle.com

Magic Mesh www.magicmesh.com

Magic Scraps www.magicscraps.com

Making Memories www.makingmemories.com

Marks of Distinction www.marks-of-distinction.com

Marvy www.marvy.com

May Arts www.mayarts.com

McGill www.mcgillinc.com

Me & My Big Ideas www.meandmybigideas.com

Mother Rubberstamps www.motherrubber.com

Mrs. Grossman www.mrsgrossmans.com

Nellie Snellen www.nelliesnellen.com

Offray www.offray.com

Paper Inspirations www.paperinspirations.com

Paper Parachute www.paperparachute.com

Creative Paperclay www.paperclay.com

Pebbles.com www.pebbles.com

Penny Black www.pennyblackinc.com

Polyform www.sculpey.com

Posh Impressions www.poshimpressions.com

Pressed Petals www.pressedpetals.com

Prima www.primamarketinginc.com

Prismacolor www.prismacolor.com

PSX www.sierra-enterprises.com

Quilled Creations www.quilledcreations.com

Ranger www.rangerink.com

Royal Brush www.royalbrush.com

Rubber Stamp Ave. www.rubberstampave.com

Rubber Stampede www.rubberstampede.com

Sandi Miller www.usartquest.com

Savvy www.savvystamps.com

Scenic Route Paper www.scenicroutepaper.com

Spellbinders www.spellbinders.us

Stamp in the Hand www.astampinthehand.com

Stampboard www.stampbord.com

Stampers Anonymous   www.stampersanonymous.com

Stampfrancisco www.stampfrancisco.com

Stamping Sensations stampingsensations.com

Stampscapes www.stampscapes.com

Sunday International www.sundayint.com

The Paper Co. www.papercompany.com

The Paper Cut www.thepapercut.com

Third Coast Rubberstamps www.thirdcoastrs.com

Tombow www.tombowusa.com

Tsukineko www.tsukineko.com

USArtQuest, Inc. www.usartquest.com

Versamark www.tsukineko.com

Woodware Craft Collection www.woodware.co.uk

Wordsworth www.wordsworthstamps.com

Worldwin www.worldwinpapers.com

Wrights www.wrights.com

Zsiage www.zsiage.com

A NOTE ON SUPPLIERS

Usually, you can find the supplies you need for making the projects in Lark books at your local craft supply store, discount mart, home improvement center, or retail shop relevant to the topic of the book. Occasionally, however, you may need to buy materials or tools from specialty suppliers. In order to provide you with the most up-to-date information, we have created a listing of suppliers on our website, which we update on a regular basis. Visit us at www.larkbooks.com, click on "Sources," and then search for the relevant materials. You can also search by book title, vendor, and author name. Additionally, you can search for supply sources located in or near your town by entering your zip code. You will find numerous companies listed, with the web address and/or mailing address and phone number.

Metric Conversion Chart

Inches	Millimeters (mm)/ Centimeters (cm)
⅛	3 mm
³⁄₁₆	5 mm
¼	6 mm
⁵⁄₁₆	8 mm
⅜	9.5 mm
⁷⁄₁₆	1.1 cm
½	1.3 cm
⁹⁄₁₆	1.4 cm
⅝	1.6 cm
¹¹⁄₁₆	1.7 cm
¾	1.9 cm
¹³⁄₁₆	2.1 cm
⅞	2.2 cm
¹⁵⁄₁₆	2.4 cm
1	2.5 cm
1½	3.8 cm
2	5 cm
2½	6.4 cm
3	7.6 cm
3½	8.9 cm
4	10.2 cm
4½	11.4 cm
5	12.7 cm
5½	14 cm
6	15.2 cm
6½	16.5 cm
7	17.8 cm
7½	19 cm
8	20.3 cm

Inches	Millimeters (mm)/ Centimeters (cm)
8½	21.6 cm
9	22.9 cm
9½	24.1 cm
10	25.4 cm
10½	26.7 cm
11	27.9 cm
11½	29.2 cm
12	30.5 cm
12½	31.8 cm
13	33 cm
13½	34.3 cm
14	35.6 cm
14½	36.8 cm
15	38.1 cm
15½	39.4 cm
16	40.6 cm
16½	41.9 cm
17	43.2 cm
17½	44.5 cm
18	45.7 cm
18½	47 cm
19	48.3 cm
19½	49.5 cm
20	50.8 cm
20½	52 cm
21	53.3 cm
21½	54.6 cm
22	55 cm
22½	57.2 cm

Inches	Millimeters (mm)/ Centimeters (cm)
23	58.4 cm
23½	59.7 cm
24	61 cm
24½	62.2 cm
25	63.5 cm
25½	64.8 cm
26	66 cm
26½	67.3 cm
27	68.6 cm
27½	69.9 cm
28	71.1 cm
28½	72.4 cm
29	73.7 cm
29½	74.9 cm
30	76.2 cm
30½	77.5 cm
31	78.7 cm
31½	80 cm
32	81.3 cm
32½	82.6 cm
33	83.8 cm
33½	85 cm
34	86.4 cm
34½	87.6 cm
35	88.9 cm
35½	90.2 cm
36	91.4 cm

About the Author

President of USArtQuest, Inc.—a manufacturer and distributor of fine art and craft materials—Susan Pickering Rothamel also teaches traditional and cutting-edge techniques using a variety of mediums. Her expertise runs from furniture making, assemblage, and altered-art forms to collage, watercolor and acrylic painting, and of course, greeting cards. She is the author of *The Art of Paper Collage* (Sterling/Chapelle, 2001) and *The Encyclopedia of Scrapbooking Tools and Techniques* (Sterling/Chapelle, 2005). Susan enthusiastically fills her days with product and technique development, teaching, and bountiful creativity.

Acknowledgments

Your Kindness is So Appreciated.

Dear Ray,
Working with such a talented and kind editor has been the most delightful experience an author could have. Thank you! Your patience and organizational skills are above and beyond the call of duty, and so appreciated.

You and your team have been amazing and it made writing this book such a pleasure. I hope we have the opportunity to have a long and valued friendship, with many books to come.

Most kindly,
Sue

Thank you for all you do!

Dear Frankie,
Your friendship means so much to me, more than just a few words here can express, but I'll try.

Thank you, for the enormity of your support in creating so many beautiful cards for this book. Just as importantly, for making sure we ate so well throughout the last several months! You sure are a wonderful cook, a singularly talented artist, and this girl's heartfelt friend.

Thank you from my heart.
Love, Sue

Congratulations!

Dear Julie,
We did it! Congratulations on making it through yet another encyclopedic book. I'll bet you'd never thought we could do it again? It's been so nice working with you and I want to thank you for your thoughtful effort, your time and the talent you've given this project.

You're the best!

Love,
Sue

Your Love fills my Heart

Dearest Dave,
You truly are the most patient soul. Thank you, dearheart, for giving me the time and space I needed to pull this one out. As usual, you've gone over and beyond the call of duty. You're a wonderful man and you have blessed my life.

I love you.
Sue

Artist Credits

Ahlstrom, Ramie—129, 282

Allen, Kit—51

Anderson, Beverly—3, 5, 58, 62–64, 86, 156, 183, 204, 221, 228, 238–239

Barkley, Carolyn—176

Bartkowski, Allie—56, 91, 133, 168, 195–196, 257, 269, 284

Berndt, Deb—45, 69, 91, 103–104, 122, 164, 173, 215, 226, 258–259, 271, 280–281

Bethany, Tera—256

Bodie, Betsie—31

Brunelle, Virginie-144

Burchill, Liz—97, 126, 200, 263–264, 266

Burt, Jan—54

Chlebana, Cathy—44, 82–83

Coombs, John Eric—54, 56

Davenport, Julie—5, 22, 24–26, 29, 31, 38–40, 44, 48, 55, 59, 62, 70, 90–91, 108, 117, 119, 125, 156, 158–159, 163, 171, 174, 183–184, 187–188, 191, 197–198, 201–204, 207, 215–218, 220, 225, 237, 244–246, 257, 259, 271, 288–289

Doucette, Kathy—105

Dutton, PJ—68, 168

Everse, Lea—47, 71, 78

Fioretti, Frankie—3, 5, 26, 28–30, 35, 37–38, 41, 43, 52–53, 55, 59, 62, 64–65, 69, 71–74, 79–81, 85–86, 91, 93, 95–96, 102, 106–109, 111–112, 115–116, 118–122, 130–134, 137, 139, 142–145, 148–152, 155, 160–162, 164, 166, 169–170, 172, 176–177, 179–180, 185–186, 189, 193, 201, 203, 208–209, 212, 216, 218, 226, 234–235, 245–247, 250, 252, 257, 267–270, 272–273, 279, 282–283, 285–287, 290

Fremuth, Julie—59

Gill, Jane—5, 192, 250, 268

Glidden, Susan—32

Gruenig, Dee—22–23, 28, 47, 58, 63, 131, 136, 145, 147, 165, 183, 199, 219, 223, 227, 230, 246

Haefke, Joyce—22, 23, 135

Harazin, Gene—267

Lemke, Jill—54, 88

Locke, Amy—103, 222, 252, 257

Loomis, Cristina—182

Mason, Lori—37, 238

McClung, Pam—130

McCorkle, Toni—113, 213

McGraw, Mary Jo—68

Miller, Sandi—56, 63, 129, 181, 249

Morrison, Summer Rose—128

Mullett, Fred—66, 233, 263

Nakagawa, Kevin—64, 122, 209–211, 228

Nichols, Marlene—182

Paper Pickle Ladies, Kim & Kelly—238

Pickering, Pam—182

Puri—36

Rabinowe, Victoria—102

Reese, Linda—215

Revetta, Allison—178

Roland, Cindy—46, 55, 62, 90, 108, 112, 134, 155, 157, 226–227, 242, 251

Rothamel, Susan Pickering—3, 6–7, 27, 33–34, 44, 55–56, 60, 62, 70, 74–77, 79, 81, 85, 87, 89, 100, 114, 116, 120, 125–127, 136, 139–140, 146, 149, 158, 162–163, 167, 179, 185, 188, 191, 198, 201, 207, 213–214, 221–222, 224–225, 229, 231, 234–235, 241–242, 247, 252, 255, 264, 284, 295–296

Sarine, Linda—23

Schwartz-Herbert, Heather—242

Sewald, Liz—23, 27, 29–32, 34, 39, 41, 44, 46, 49, 52, 54, 62, 67, 74, 87, 92–94, 96, 102–103, 105, 109, 111, 115, 117, 119, 142, 144, 151–153, 157, 159, 162–163, 186, 205–206, 217, 221, 235, 240, 247, 250–252, 254, 258, 263

Shackleford, Jean Harley—243

Snellen, Nellie—194

Stover, Connie—68

Tan, Flora—45

Taormina, Grace—93

Thiewes, Cy—264–265

Tracy, Susie—130

Weinbrg, Suze—47, 154

Weldon, Sara—227

Wind, Debi—248

Woodman, Sue—66, 74, 80, 86, 104–105, 142, 144, 184, 256–257, 259

Cards on pages 66, 80, 256, and 259 were created with stamps from House-Mouse Designs Inc., P.O. Box 48, Williston, VT 05495. Stamp images © House-Mouse Designs.

Index